Bahamas

Primary Social Studies 4

Workbook

Lisa Greenstein

Acknowledgements

The Publisher expresses gratitude to Ms Jeannelle Antoine-Thomas for her assistance and guidance in the preparation of this book.

The Publishers would like to thank the following for permission to reproduce copyright material:

Text acknowledgements
pp 16–17 Columbus, Christopher. *The Diary of Christopher Columbus's First Voyage to America, 1492–1493.*

Photo acknowledgements
p. 4 cc © Vilna Robotav 3d/stock.adobe.com; p. 5 tr © Fire Wings/stock.adobe.com; p. 5 cr © Sr nNicholl/stock.adobe.com; p. 6 cl © Street And Light/Alamy Stock Photo; p. 6 cc © Tania Delmonte/Shutterstock.com; p. 6 cc © Frantisek Hojdysz/stock.adobe.com; p. 6 cr © Anna Klepatckaya/Shutterstock.com; p. 6 cr © Macau/stock.adobe.com; p. 8 cc © Asma Samoh/Shutterstock.com; p. 12 tc © Said Auita/stock.adobe.com; p. 12 tl © Daboost/stock.adobe.com; p. 12 bc © Said Auita/stock.adobe.com; p. 14 cl © Zcy/stock.adobe.com; p. 14 cc © Orly Design/stock.adobe.com; p. 14 cc © Pixel Robot/stock.adobe.com; p. 14 cc © Pixel Robot/stock.adobe.com; p. 14 cr © Alfazet Chronicles/stock.adobe.com; p. 15 tr © The History Collection/Alamy Stock Photo/Getty Images; p. 16 tr © Ullstein bild Dtl./ullstein bild via Getty Images; p. 6 cc, p. 19 cc, p. 26 bc, p. 27 cc, p. 39 cc © Lili Graphie/stock.adobe.com; p. 20 br © WENN Rights Ltd/Alamy Stock Photo; p. 25 cc © Antique Images/stock.adobe.com; p. 25 bc © Archivist/stock.adobe.com; p. 28 tr © Photravel Ru/Shutterstock.com; p. 29 tr © Macro Vector/stock.adobe.com; p. 30 cc © Adrian Hillman/stock.adobe.com; p. 31 tc © Pilarts/stock.adobe.com; p. 35 cc © Siberian Art/stock.adobe.com; p. 38 tr © Nasa Image Collection/Alamy Stock Photo; p. 41 cc © Vector V stocker/stock.adobe.com; p. 41 cc © Natalia/stock.adobe.com; p. 41 cc © Natalia/stock.adobe.com; p. 41 cc © Aleks Angel/stock.adobe.com; p. 41 cc © Tigatelu/stock.adobe.com; p. 41 cc © Onyxprj/stock.adobe.com; p. 45 cl © Alexe/stock.adobe.com; p. 45 cc © Tami Freed/stock.adobe.com; p. 45 cr © TO Images/stock.adobe.com; p. 45 cl © Henri Koskinen/stock.adobe.com; p. 45 cc © Pbr Images Peter B Ryan/Shutterstock.com; p. 45 cr © Laura Pashkevich/stock.adobe.com; p. 45 bl © Paul James Bannerman/stock.adobe.com; p. 45 bc © Fabricio UZ/stock.adobe.com; p. 45 br © Anake/stock.adobe.com; p. 47 cc © Andrei/stock.adobe.com; p. 54 tl, p. 54 tr © I Jacky/stock.adobe.com; p. 54 cl, p. 55 cr © Obertsre/stock.adobe.com; p. 54 cl, p. 55 cr © Kuzmick/stock.adobe.com; p. 54 cl, p. 55 cr © Michele Cozzolino/Shutterstock.com; p. 54 cl, p. 55 cr © Doomu/Shutterstock.com; p. 54 cl, p. 55 cr © Slinkerton 15/stock.adobe.com; p. 54 cl, p. 55 cr © Coprid/stock.adobe.com; p. 54 bl, p. 55 br © Irina Fischer/stock.adobe.com; p. 54 bc © Michael Flippo/stock.adobe.com; p. 54 bc © David Franklin/stock.adobe.com; p. 54 bc © Pixel Shot/stock.adobe.com; p. 54 br © Zakharov Evgeniy/stock.adobe.com; p. 61 tr © Johan 10/stock.adobe.com; p. 62 cc © Archivist/stock.adobe.com; p. 62 bc © Granger Historical Picture Archive/Alamy Stock Photo; p. 63 tr © Gustavo Frazao/stock.adobe.com; p. 66 cc © Yblaz/stock.adobe.com; p. 76 tr © Ekaterina/stock.adobe.com; p. 78 cl © Klyaksun/stock.adobe.com; p. 78 cl © Pasko Maksim/stock.adobe.com; p. 78 cl © Shirokuma Design/stock.adobe.com; p. 104 cr © Street and Light/Alamy Stock Photo; p. 105 tr © Svetlana Sf/Shutterstock.com; p. 107 br © Andriy Dykun/stock.adobe.com; p. 108 tr © Charles Stirling Travel/Alamy Stock Photo; p. 111 tc © Blue Orange Studio/stock.adobe.com.

t = top, b = bottom, l = left, r = right, c = centre

Every effort has been made to trace all copyright holders, but if any have been inadvertently overlooked, the Publishers will be pleased to make the necessary arrangements at the first opportunity.

Although every effort has been made to ensure that website addresses are correct at time of going to press, Hodder Education cannot be held responsible for the content of any website mentioned in this book. It is sometimes possible to find a relocated web page by typing in the address of the home page for a website in the URL window of your browser.

Hachette UK's policy is to use papers that are natural, renewable and recyclable products and made from wood grown in well-managed forests and other controlled sources. The logging and manufacturing processes are expected to conform to the environmental regulations of the country of origin.

Orders: please contact Hachette UK Distribution, Hely Hutchinson Centre, Milton Road, Didcot, Oxfordshire, OX11 7HH.
Telephone: +44 (0)1235 827827. Email education@hachette.co.uk
Lines are open from 9 a.m. to 5 p.m., Monday to Friday. You can also order through our website: www.hoddereducation.com

ISBN: 9781398380288

© Lisa Greenstein 2023

First published in 2023 by

Hodder Education

An Hachette UK Company

Carmelite House

50 Victoria Embankment

London EC4Y 0DZ

www.hoddereducation.com

Impression number   10 9 8 7 6 5 4 3 2 1

Year   2027 2026 2025 2024 2023

All rights reserved. Apart from any use permitted under UK copyright law, no part of this publication may be reproduced or transmitted in any form or by any means, electronic or mechanical, including photocopying and recording, or held within any information storage and retrieval system, without permission in writing from the publisher or under licence from the Copyright Licensing Agency Limited. Further details of such licences (for reprographic reproduction) may be obtained from the Copyright Licensing Agency Limited, www.cla.co.uk

Cover photo © panya99/stock.adobe.com

Illustrations by Vian Oelofsen, Stéphan Theron

Typeset in FS Albert 12/16 by IO Publishing CC

Printed in Spain

A catalogue record for this title is available from the British Library.

Contents

How to use this book — 4

Chapter 1 History and heritage

1. National pride and identity — 5
2. Our ancestors — 14
3. Slavery and the Middle Passage — 24

Chapter 2 Geography

4. Working with maps — 29
5. Geography of The Bahamas — 38

Chapter 3 Economics and resources

6. Natural resources — 43
7. Tourism in The Bahamas — 57
8. Transport and communication — 71
9. Farming and fishing — 78

Chapter 4 Government

10. Our leaders — 80
11. Rights and responsibilities — 87

Chapter 5 Culture

12. Our people, our heritage — 99
13. Holidays and celebrations — 104
14. Foods and plants of The Bahamas — 110

How to use this book

This Workbook is full of places for you to draw, doodle, colour, and decorate, as well as write and make notes. The activities here will help you learn as you work through your textbook for this year. You will need a pencil, eraser and some coloured pencils or markers. Some of the things you will do in this Workbook:

- ✅ Summarise key concepts
- ✅ Define key words
- ✅ Complete information tables
- ✅ Brainstorm ideas
- ✅ Draw mind maps
- ✅ Present information in a flow chart
- ✅ Label a diagram
- ✅ Draw a picture
- ✅ Plan or record research
- ✅ Draw a graph
- ✅ Use a map
- ✅ Write a summary
- ✅ Reflect on your own experience, opinion or views on a topic.

1. National pride and identity

CHAPTER 1: History and heritage

I am a proud Bahamian

The Bahamas is an **archipelago**. That means our country is made up of many small islands. There are about 700 islands in our country, of which 30 are **inhabited**. The people who are citizens in our archipelagic nation are known as **Bahamians**. It is important for all Bahamians to have a sense of **national pride** and **patriotism**.

1. In your own words, write the definitions of these terms.

   key words

   archipelago ....
   national pride ....
   patriotism ....

2. Describe how each picture demonstrates patriotic behaviour.

5

Chapter 1 History and heritage

Our culture

When we talk about the **culture** of a country, we think of many different aspects. The language, music, food, dance, festivals and traditions are just some of these.

1. In each box below, write ideas or examples of Bahamian culture.

Language

Music

Food

Dancing and festivals

Traditional sayings or beliefs

2. What does being Bahamian mean to you? Write a poem or a paragraph expressing your own ideas.

_____
_____
_____
_____
_____

Unit 1 National pride and identity

3. Choose another island from The Bahamas chain to compare with the island you live on. List any similarities and differences about different aspects of life on the two islands.

My island in The Bahamas: _____

Another Bahamian island: _____

- People
- Music, dance and culture
- Places
- Events
- **SIMILARITIES AND DIFFERENCES**
- Language and sayings
- Food and drinks

Chapter 1 History and heritage

Our national crest

The **national crest** of The Bahamas is also known as the **Coat of Arms** of our country. It is made up of **symbols** that represent important parts of our culture and history.

1. Identify each symbol on the national crest. Write what the significance of each symbol is.

8

Unit 1 National pride and identity

2 Look at the crests for all the major islands in The Bahamas in your Student's Book. Imagine that you have been asked to develop a new crest for your own island..

    a In this space, brainstorm ideas for important symbols of your island. Think about important places, plants and animals, people and natural resources of your island. Then use these to design your new crest.

_____
_____
_____
_____
_____
_____
_____

    b In this space, design your crest.

Chapter 1 History and heritage

Taking pride in our environment

1. Keeping our environment clean helps us to take pride in our community and our country. Think about the ways we do this. For each place, write what we can do to keep it clean and presentable.

Unit 1 National pride and identity

2. Label this picture of children cleaning their classroom.

- wipe tables
- use the bin
- pack away
- wipe walls
- sweep floor
- stack papers neatly
- organise

3. Organise a school or community clean-up day. Write here which area in your school or community needs to be cleaned up, and why you think it is important to improve this area.

_____
_____
_____
_____

Chapter 1 History and heritage

The national pledge and anthem

1. Complete the national pledge here.

"I ⬚ my ⬚ to the ⬚ and to the Commonwealth of ⬚

For which it stands, one people ⬚ in ⬚ and ⬚."

2. Below are the words of the national anthem, which was written by Timothy Gibson. Practise singing it with your class. Decorate it by adding symbols of life in The Bahamas.

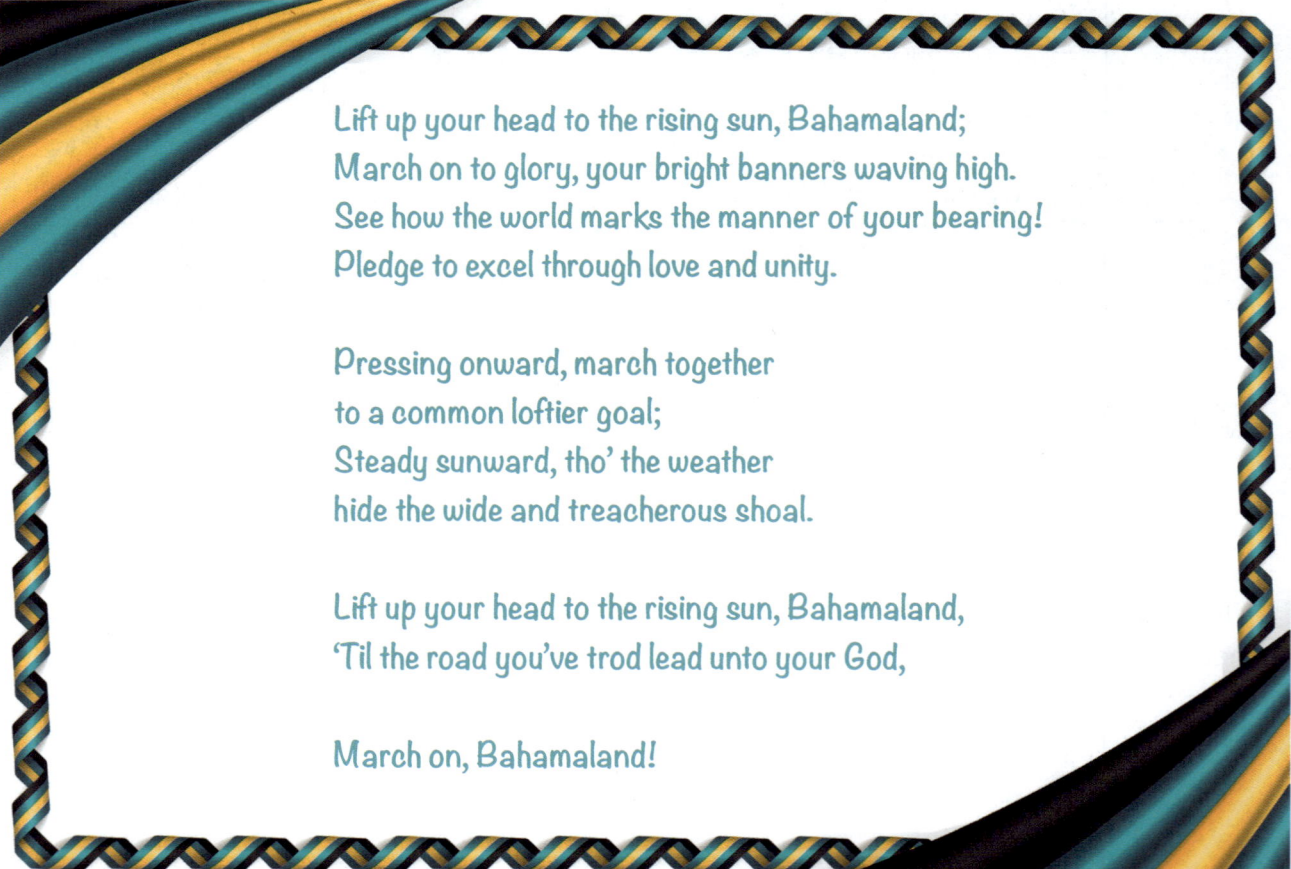

Lift up your head to the rising sun, Bahamaland;
March on to glory, your bright banners waving high.
See how the world marks the manner of your bearing!
Pledge to excel through love and unity.

Pressing onward, march together
to a common loftier goal;
Steady sunward, tho' the weather
hide the wide and treacherous shoal.

Lift up your head to the rising sun, Bahamaland,
'Til the road you've trod lead unto your God,

March on, Bahamaland!

3 Draw a cartoon strip to illustrate the national anthem.

2 Our ancestors

Who were the Lucayans?

The earliest **indigenous** people of The Bahamas were the Lucayans. They were related to the Tainos who lived on other islands in the Caribbean. The Tainos originally came from South America, from where they spread to the islands of Cuba and Hispaniola (now Haiti and the Dominican Republic). Between 700 and 1500 AD, The Bahamas was the home of the peaceful Lucayan people, with about 40,000 Lucayans spread out over the larger islands.

They spoke the Taíno language, and had their own system of **religion** and **government**. The leader of the Lucayans was known as the cacique. The Lucayans lived in peace and **freedom** before the European explorers came and took The Bahamas as a colony.

The Lucayans were a fishing community, and lived mostly on shellfish, although they also farmed crops such as cassava and aloe. They also grew cotton and used it for trading with other islands.

shellfish

cotton

kingfish

conch shell

aloe

Several families lived together in each house, which was built very simply from poles and thatch. Archaeologists believe the households were matriarchal (led by the women of the house).

Unit 2 Our ancestors

Artifacts show that the Lucayans used stone and animal bones to create tools. They made carved canoes and furniture. A **duho** was a special type of ceremonial chair, carved from wood, often showing a man on his stomach or on all fours.

① These words all come from the Taíno language. Choose three of the words that we still use today. Write what it means and draw a small picture to illustrate each word.

- hammock
- iguana
- maize
- tobacco
- barbecue
- canoe
- caiman
- mangrove

② Write definitions of these words.

key words

freedom ....

colony ....

religion ....

Chapter 1 History and heritage

The arrival of Columbus and the destruction of the Lucayans

In 1492, the Spanish explorer Christopher Columbus arrived in The Bahamas. The Lucayans were welcoming and generous to the explorers, but the arrival of the Europeans would bring terrible destruction to the indigenous people of the islands.

The only written records we have from this time are from Columbus's diary. These accounts tell us a bit about Lucayan life, but also about the Europeans' attitude towards the local people they met. Within 25 years, the Lucayan population had been destroyed. Many were killed or worked to death by the Spanish, or kidnapped for the slave trade.

A painting of Columbus's arrival. Historians believe he landed on Watling's Island.

1. Read these extracts from Columbus's diary. Use the information to draw your own illustration on the next page of one of the scenes described.

> ".. reached an islet of the Lucayos, which was called Guanahani in the language of the Indians… Later they came swimming to the ships' launches where we were and brought us parrots and cotton thread in balls and javelins and many other things, and they traded them to us for other things which we gave them, such as small glass beads and bells.
>
> All of them go around as naked as their mother bore them; and the women also, although I did not see more than one quite young girl. And all those that I saw were young people… with handsome bodies and good faces. Their hair coarse – almost like the tail of a horse – and short. They wear their hair down over their eyebrows except for a little in the back which they wear long and never cut
>
> … And some of them paint their faces, and some the whole body, and some of them only the eyes, and some of them only the nose.
>
> They do not carry arms nor are they acquainted with them, because I showed them swords and they took them by the edge and through ignorance cut themselves. They have no iron. Their javelins are shafts without iron and some of them have at the end a fish tooth …
>
> … I saw some who had marks of wounds on their bodies and I made signs to them asking them what they were; and they showed me how people from other islands nearby came there and tried to take them, and how they defended themselves.

Unit 2 Our ancestors

② How do these diary extracts show you that the Lucayans were a peace-loving people?
_____
_____
_____

③ What did Columbus notice about the appearance of the Lucayan people?
_____
_____
_____

④ Imagine that you were a Lucayan and saw the Spanish explorers arriving on your island. Write an account from the Lucayan point of view, describing the appearance of the explorers and what they brought.
_____
_____
_____
_____
_____
_____
_____
_____
_____
_____

17

Chapter 1 History and heritage

The Eleutherian Adventurers

Around 1647, a group of 70 English Puritans set sail from Bermuda to The Bahamas with Captain William Sayle. In Bermuda, the British king had ordered that everyone had to worship in the Anglican Church. This group wanted to be free to worship in their own churches. They arrived at an island in The Bahamas which they named Eleuthera, Greek for freedom.

The settlers brought food, tools and seeds. However, the soil was very poor so it was difficult to grow crops. They survived by eating berries and fishing. Life on the island was very difficult, and many settlers left. Some moved to another island they called Sayle's Island, which they later named Providence. Today, this island is called New Providence.

1. Some of the surnames of the Eleutheran adventurers are listed below. Look at a map of New Providence. Which places still have names that come from these settlers?

   Albury   Bethel   Bullard   Butler
   Cartwright   Knowles   Nottage   Pinder
   Sands   Russell   Thompson   Williams

2. Talk to your family members. Does your family, or any other family in your community, have names or surnames that date back to the Eleutheran Adventurers? List other family names from this time.

3 Imagine that you were alive at the time of the Eleutheran Adventurers. You are working for a community newspaper, and you decide to interview Captain Sayle or Butler. Think of the questions you would ask, and imagine their answers. Write your interview with them here.

Chapter 1 History and heritage

The arrival of the Loyalists

By the 1780s, the United States had gained independence. It was no longer a colony of Britain. However, a group called the Loyalists wanted to remain loyal to the king of England. They set sail from America to The Bahamas. At this time, The Bahamas was still a British colony.

The Loyalists established cotton **plantations**. A plantation is a large area of land where the natural vegetation was cleared in order to grow crops such as cotton, sugar, coffee, tobacco and cocoa. These crops earned a lot of money for the ruling empire. A plantation usually had a large house for the plantation owner and their family, enormous fields for the crops, and enslaved people who had to live on the plantation and work in the fields and the house.

In The Bahamas, the Loyalists grew huge amounts of cotton, which was exported to America. When the enslaved people were not working in the fields, they raked salt from the salt pans.

Not all Loyalists were plantation owners. Some were fishermen in Abaco and Eleuthera.

Mostly, the Loyalists were Anglican Christians. They built churches such as Christ Church Cathedral and St. Matthew's Anglican Church. They started schools. John Wells started a newspaper.

Christ Church Cathedral in Nassau, the oldest church in The Bahamas

Unit 2 Our ancestors

1 Complete this table comparing the Eleutheran Adventurers and the Loyalists.

	Eleutheran Adventurers	**Loyalists**
Country of origin		
Reason for coming to The Bahamas		
Religion		
Examples of surnames from this group		
Positive contributions to Bahamian history and culture		
Negative contributions to Bahamian history and culture		
Additional similarities or differences		

Chapter 1 History and heritage

❷ Choose a building on your island that was built during the time of the Loyalist plantations. Complete a ⭐fact file about this building. Draw or paste in a picture.

A building constructed by the Loyalists

- Name of building: ....
- Year of construction: ....
- Who was it built for? ....
- What was its original purpose? ....
- What is it used for today? ....
....
....

- Additional interesting facts about this building:
....
....
....
....
....
....
....
....
....
....
....

Unit 2 Our ancestors

3. Imagine what life was like for different people who lived on a plantation. Write a few sentences to show what each of these people might have said about their lives. You can also work in groups to reenact scenes from the lives of these people.

Plantation owner

Mistress of the house

House slave

Field slaves

3 Slavery and the Middle Passage

The transatlantic slave trade

> The **transatlantic slave trade** lasted for about 400 years between the 16th and 19th centuries. 'Transatlantic' means across the Atlantic Ocean. More than 11 million people were kidnapped from Africa.

1. The slave ships followed a triangular route from Europe down the west African coast, across the Atlantic to the West Indies and the east coast of North America, and then back across to Europe. They took:
   - manufactured goods such as weapons, fabrics and wine from Europe to Africa, where they would use these goods to pay for African men, women and children who had been kidnapped from their own communities
   - human cargo from Africa to the New World (the Caribbean and Americas), where they would sell the trafficked people to plantation owners in exchange for raw materials such as sugar, tobacco, cotton, coffee and cocoa
   - raw materials from the New World to Europe.

   Use this information to match each label to the correct arrow.

   enslaved African people   raw materials   manufactured goods

2. Think about what you have learnt about the Loyalists. Explain in your own words how the arrival of the Loyalists was a key event that led to slavery in The Bahamas.

   _____
   _____
   _____
   _____

This engraving shows how local mercenaries would raid African villages to kidnap people and march them to African ports, where they would be held as prisoners until they were sold and loaded onto slave ships. This stage was known as the '**First Passage**', as imprisoned Africans were marched from their homes to the coast.

The '**Middle Passage**' was the next stage of the journey, where the enslaved people travelled by ship from Africa to the Caribbean or the Americas. The enslaved people were tightly packed into the lower deck of the ship. It was horrifically overcrowded, hot and poorly ventilated, with no sanitation. Men were **shackled** together with leg-irons, and forced to remain lying down as the space was too small to allow them to sit up. Women and children were usually kept in a separate part of the ship, where they had a little more freedom to move around. However, the crew would often abuse them and treat them violently. Between 15 and 25% of the enslaved people on each ship died as a result of these conditions.

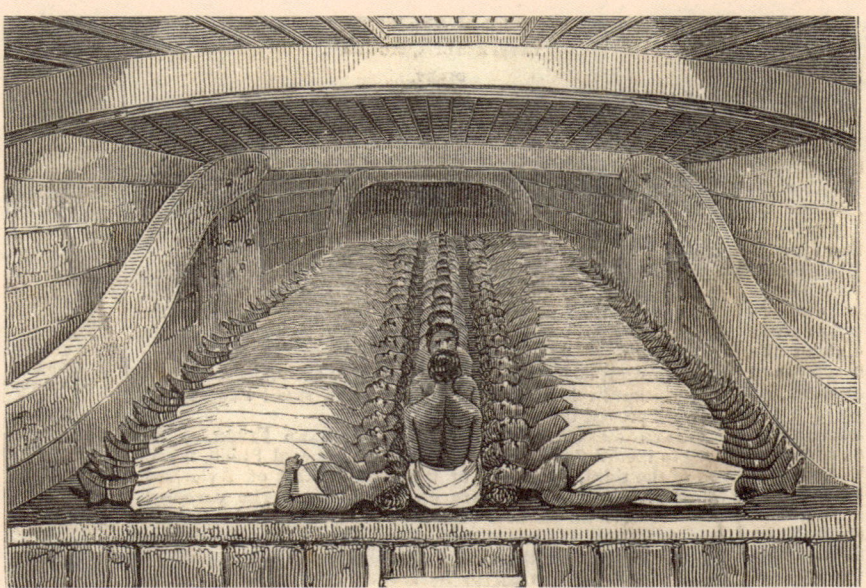

Chapter 1 History and heritage

3 Use the information from the previous page to help you write definitions of these words. You can also use a dictionary, reference book or the internet to help you.

key words

transatlantic ....

slave ....

slave trade ....

Middle Passage ....

mercenary ....

shackled ....

4 Imagine the people living at the time of the transatlantic slave trade. Imagine how life must have felt to people living in African villages and cities, to the traders and ship's crew, and to the people who were imprisoned and enslave. Choose two different people from this time. Write a diary entry or letter from each point of view.

Chapter 1 History and heritage

The influence of slavery on The Bahamas

Clifton Heritage National Park is an important heritage area in The Bahamas. Many people visit the area to enjoy the swimming on the beach, diving and snorkelling, but also to learn more about the history of the island. A tour can include a visit to the ruins of an old plantation house and slave village. Your guide can answer many questions about the history of slavery in The Bahamas.

1. Plan a visit to Clifton Heritage National Park with your class. Write here some questions you would like to ask.

2. If possible, visit the heritage site. If it is not possible, do your own research using the internet, local museum or library. Think about how life in The Bahamas today was affected by the slave trade. Write your ideas and observations here.

4 Working with maps

CHAPTER 2: Geography

Directions

The four main **cardinal directions** are **north (N)**, **south (S)**, **east (E)** and **west (W)**. On some maps, you will see these directions on a **compass rose**. This is a symbol that shows you the orientation of the map. Most maps show north at the top. Between the cardinal directions, you can find the secondary directions: **northeast (NE)**, **northwest (NW)**, **southeast (SE)** and **southwest (SW)**.

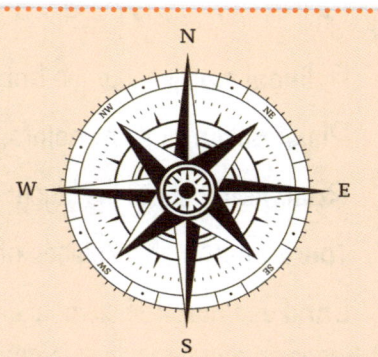

1 Complete the directions to make each statement true.

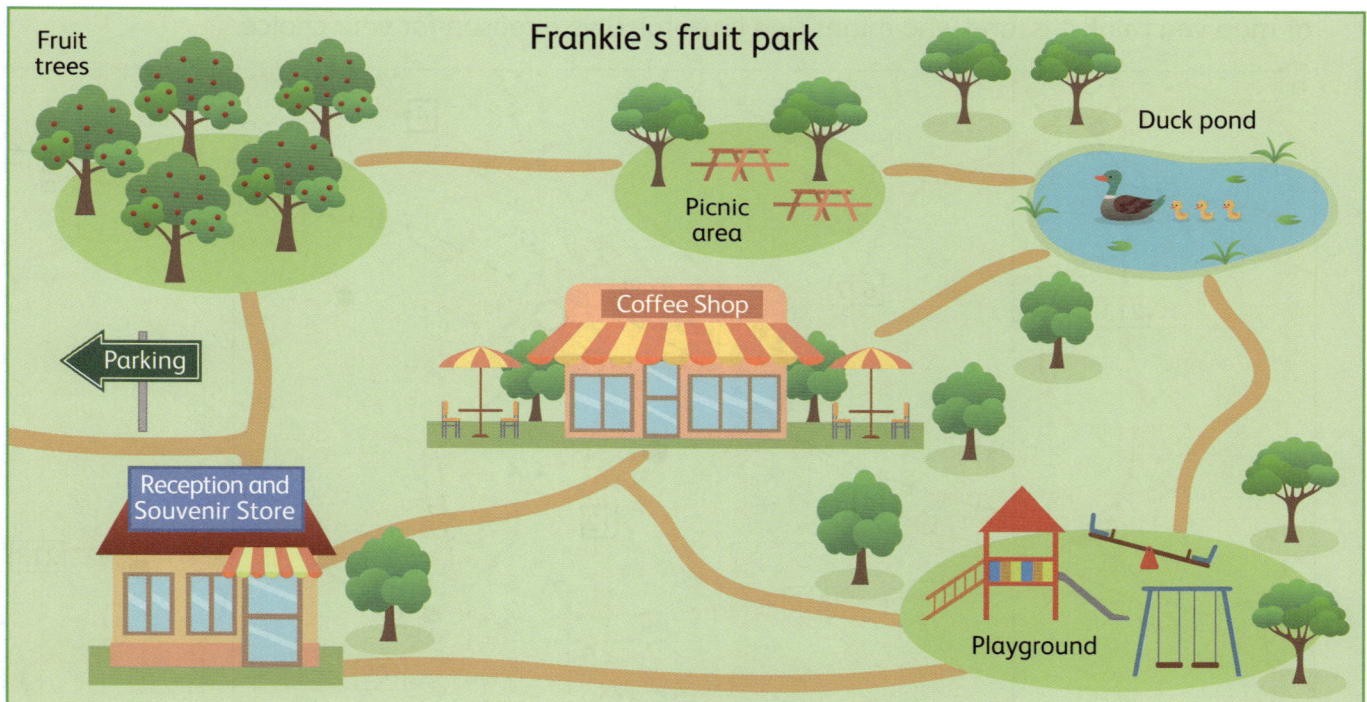

a   The fruit trees are _____ of the reception and _____ of the picnic area.
b   The playground is _____ of the duck pond.
c   The coffee shop is _____ of the souvenir store.
d   The parking area is _____ of the park.
e   To get from the playground to the coffee shop, you would walk in a _____ direction.
f   What is south of the picnic area? _____
g   What is northwest of the coffee shop? _____

Chapter 2 Geography

Different types of maps

A **map** is a diagram of a particular place on Earth. We draw maps as if we are looking directly down at the ground from above. This is called a **bird's eye view**. Maps are much smaller than the real area they represent. We use symbols to represent features in real life. Different types of maps focus on different **features**, for example:

* **Political maps** show the **borders** of countries and the locations of the main towns and cities.
* **Physical maps** show natural features, including mountains, seas, rivers and lakes.
* **Road maps** show the layout of the roads and highways.
* **Tourist maps** show places of interest for visitors, such as hotels, landmarks and visitors' **attractions**.
* **Land use maps** show how different areas are used, such as for residential areas (where people live), industry and agriculture. Some places are protected from use, such as heritage sites and nature reserves.

1. Look carefully at each map on this page and the next page. Discuss with a partner. Say what type of map you think it is, and who might find it useful. Give a reason for your choice.

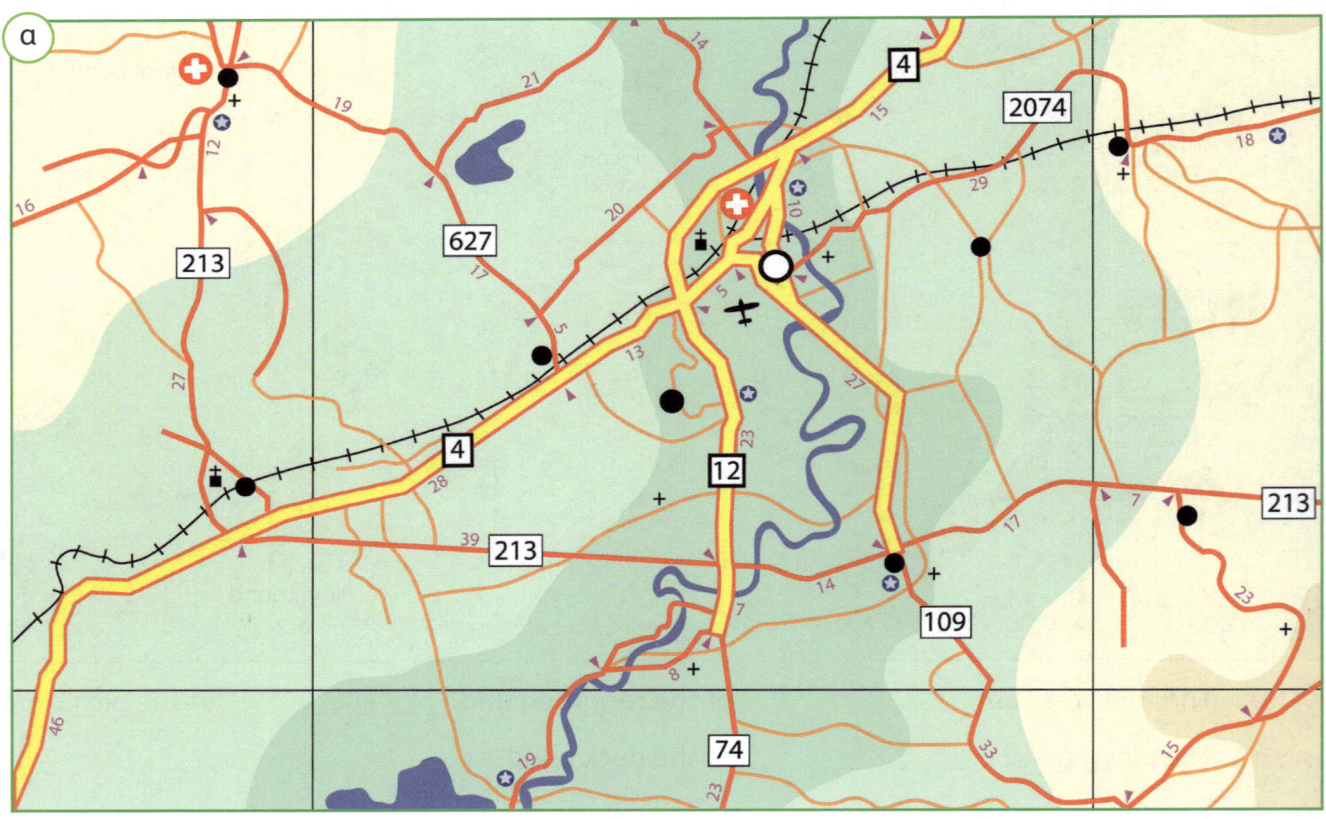

a

30

Unit 4 Working with maps

b

c

31

Chapter 2 Geography

2. Fill in N, NW, W, SW, S, SE, E and NE on the compass.

3. Use the map and the compass to help you answer the questions that follow.

a Name two islands that are south of Dominica. _____

b Which country is west of Haiti? _____

c Which country is directly north of Jamaica? _____

d Name two islands that are east of Puerto Rico. _____

4. Make up a question of your own about the map for a partner to answer.

Unit 4 Working with maps

Map scales

The **scale** of a map tells us the relationship between distances on the map and distances in real life. Different types of maps use different scales, depending on how big an area we are trying to see.

This is a **ratio scale**. It tells us that 1 cm on the map represents 100 km in real life.

1 cm : 100 km

Below is a **linear scale**. It uses a line with distance markings to show that 1 cm on the map represents 100 km in real life.

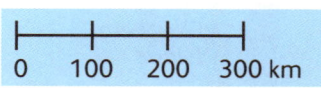

① Work with a partner. Which scale would be suitable for each type of map below?

- a map of a room in your house
- a map of a small island
- a map of your village
- a map showing some of the countries of South America
- a map of a local mall

a 1 cm = 2 km _____

b 1 cm = 1 m _____

c 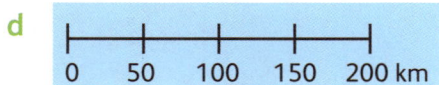 _____

d 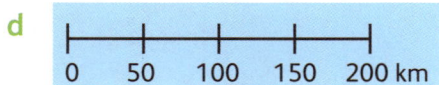 _____

e 1 cm : 1000 km _____

② Use your ruler to help you work out the real-life distance between point A and point B on each map.

a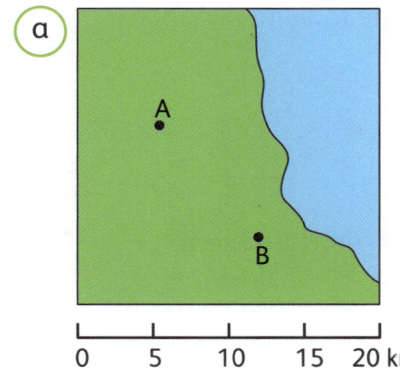

b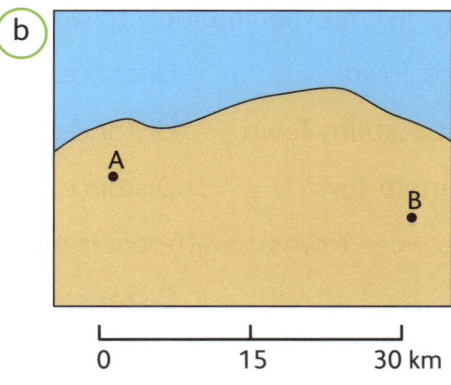

c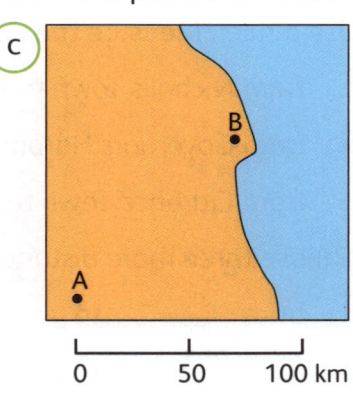

_____   _____   _____

33

Chapter 2 Geography

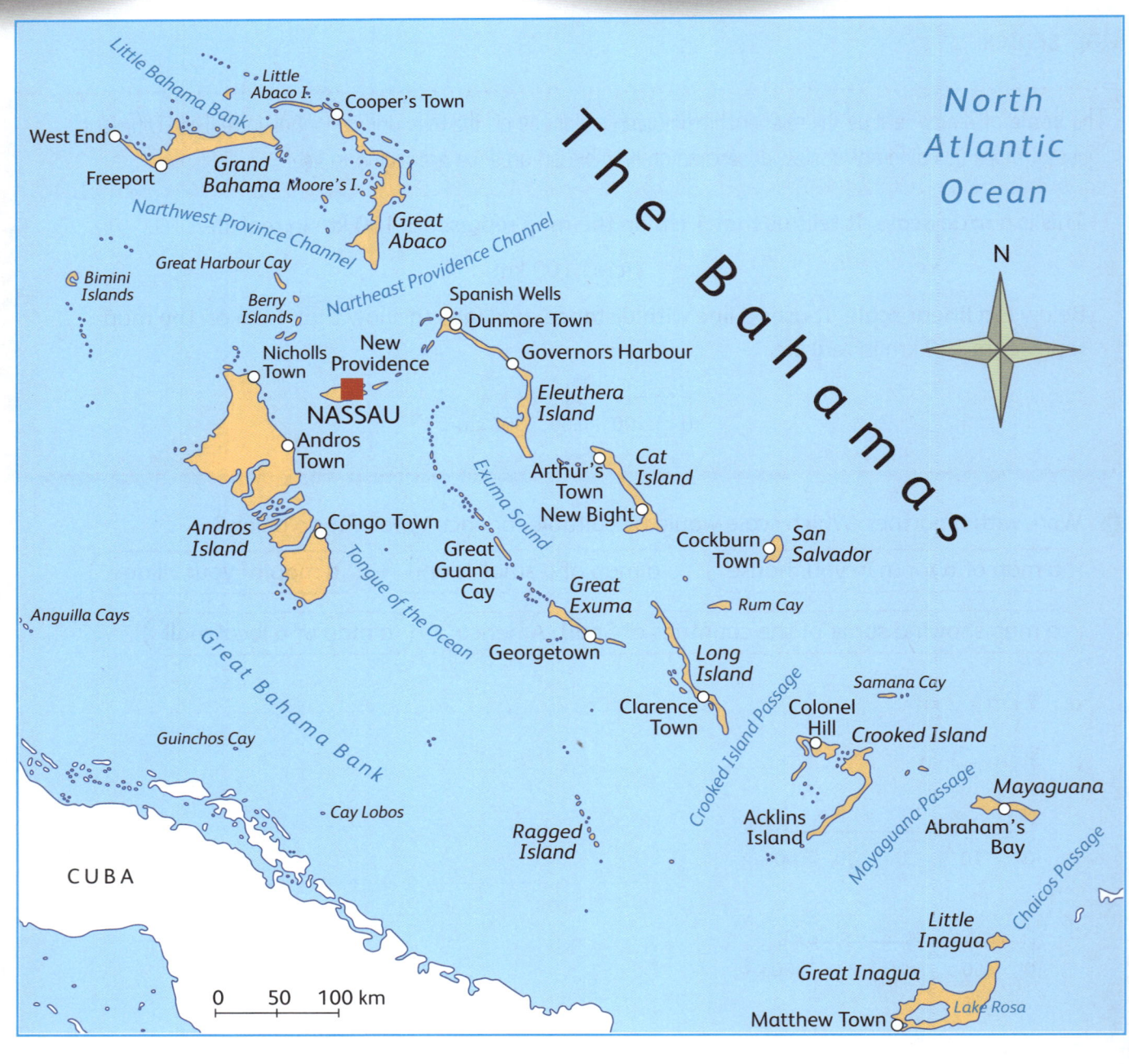

3. Write the scale of the map as a ratio. 1 cm : _____.

4. Use a ruler. Measure the distance in cm. Then multiply to work out the real-life distance.

    a from Nicholls Town to Andros Town   Distance: _____

    b from Governors Harbour to Cockburn Town   Distance: _____

    c from Clarence Town to Dunmore Town   Distance: _____

5. Choose three more distances between towns on different islands and measure them.

    a from _____ to _____   Distance: _____

    b from _____ to _____   Distance: _____

    c from _____ to _____   Distance: _____

Lines of longitude and latitude

On world maps, you can see thin lines drawn in a grid over the map. These are imaginary lines that help us to locate places on the map. **Lines of latitude** are horizontal lines running north and south of the Equator. **Lines of longitude** are vertical lines that run east and west of the Greenwich Meridian. The lines are marked in degrees (°). The islands of The Bahamas lie between latitude 20°N and 28°N, and between longitude 72°W and 80°W. The Equator is at 0° latitude, and the Greenwich Meridian is at 0° longitude.

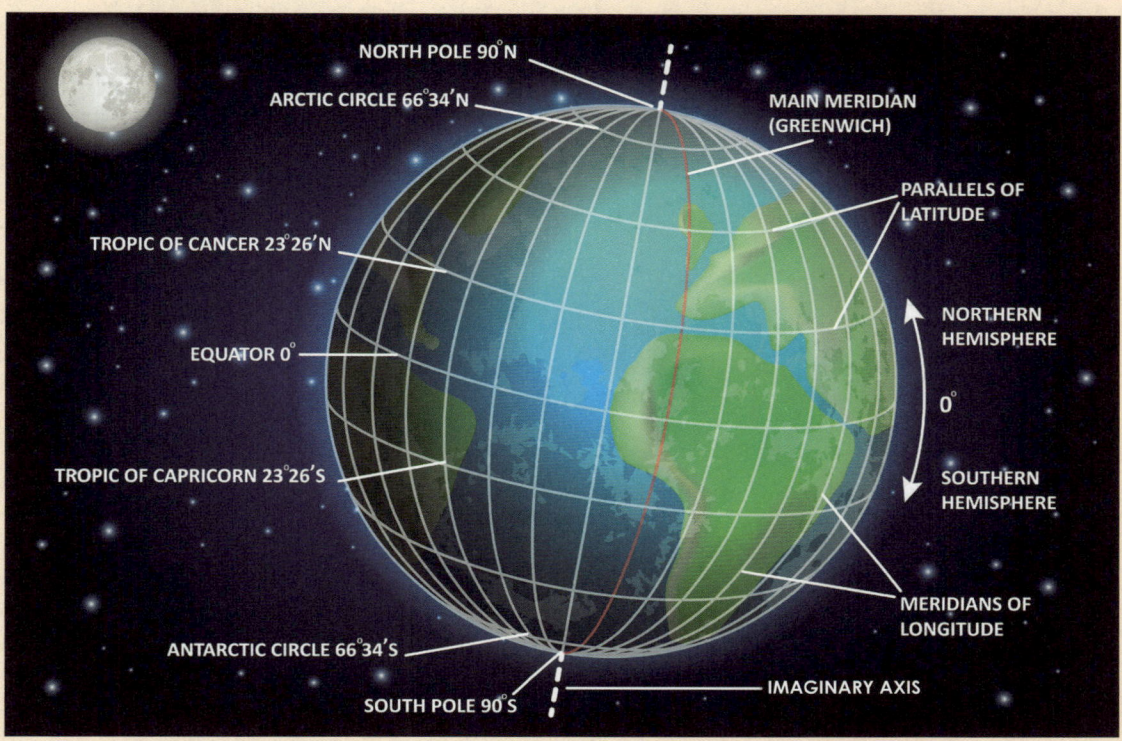

1. These sentences are incorrect. Rewrite the underlined word to correct each sentence.

   a The Tropics are lines of <u>longitude</u>.

   b The <u>Greenwich Meridian</u> is the line that divides the northern and southern hemispheres.

   c The Bahamas are located near the Tropic of <u>Capricorn</u>.

2. List four lines of latitude in order from furthest south to furthest north.

Chapter 2 Geography

3 Use the lines of latitude and longitude to identify the cities at these coordinates. You can look them up in the index of an atlas to check your answers.

a 18°N 66°W _____

b 23°N 82°W _____

c 44°N 76°W _____

4 Write the approximate grid coordinate positions of these islands:

a Barbados _____

b Aruba _____

c Abaco _____

Unit 4 Working with maps

5. Use a world map or atlas. Identify three countries that are located:

a at the Equator

b on the Tropic of Capricorn

Geography of The Bahamas

Our ocean banks

The islands of The Bahamas formed over millions of years, as limestone deposits built up to form ocean **banks** – areas of the sea which are shallower than the surrounding ocean. The Great Bahama Bank lies east of Andros. It is home to one of the world's largest barrier reefs, extending for around 140 miles. Barrier reefs are important resources as they support rich **marine life** – coral, fish and other sea life. The Little Bahama Bank is located along the north coast of Grand Bahama.

A satellite view of the coral reefs show the shoals (shallow water) around the islands as brilliant turquoise.

1. Use a map or atlas to help you label the islands of The Bahamas on this map. Label:
   a The Great Bahama Bank
   b The Little Bahama Bank
   c The southern islands: Crooked Island, Acklins, Mayaguana, Inagua and Long Cay

2. Draw the Tropic of Cancer, showing which islands it passes through.

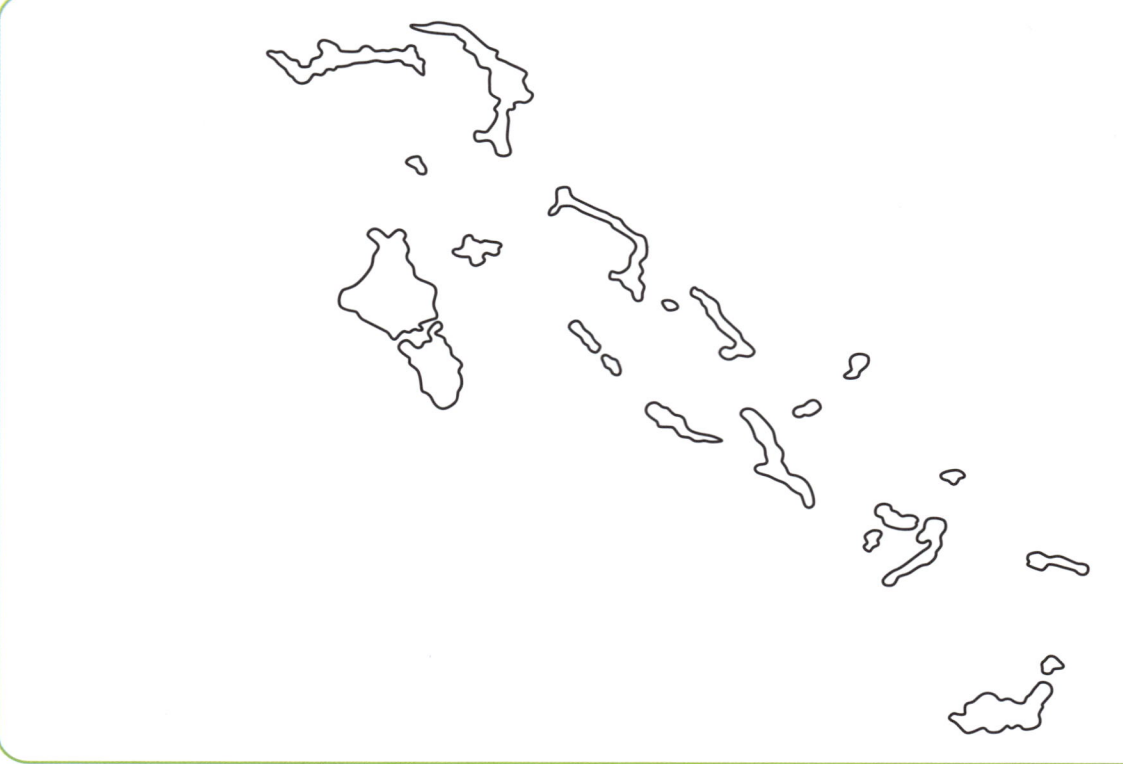

3 A mnemonic is a poem, song or sentence that helps you to remember other words. Write your own mnemonic to help you remember the names of the Bahamian islands, in order from north to south. Write it here.

Our tropical environment

Do some research about the characteristics of tropical environments. Complete this ⭐fact file.

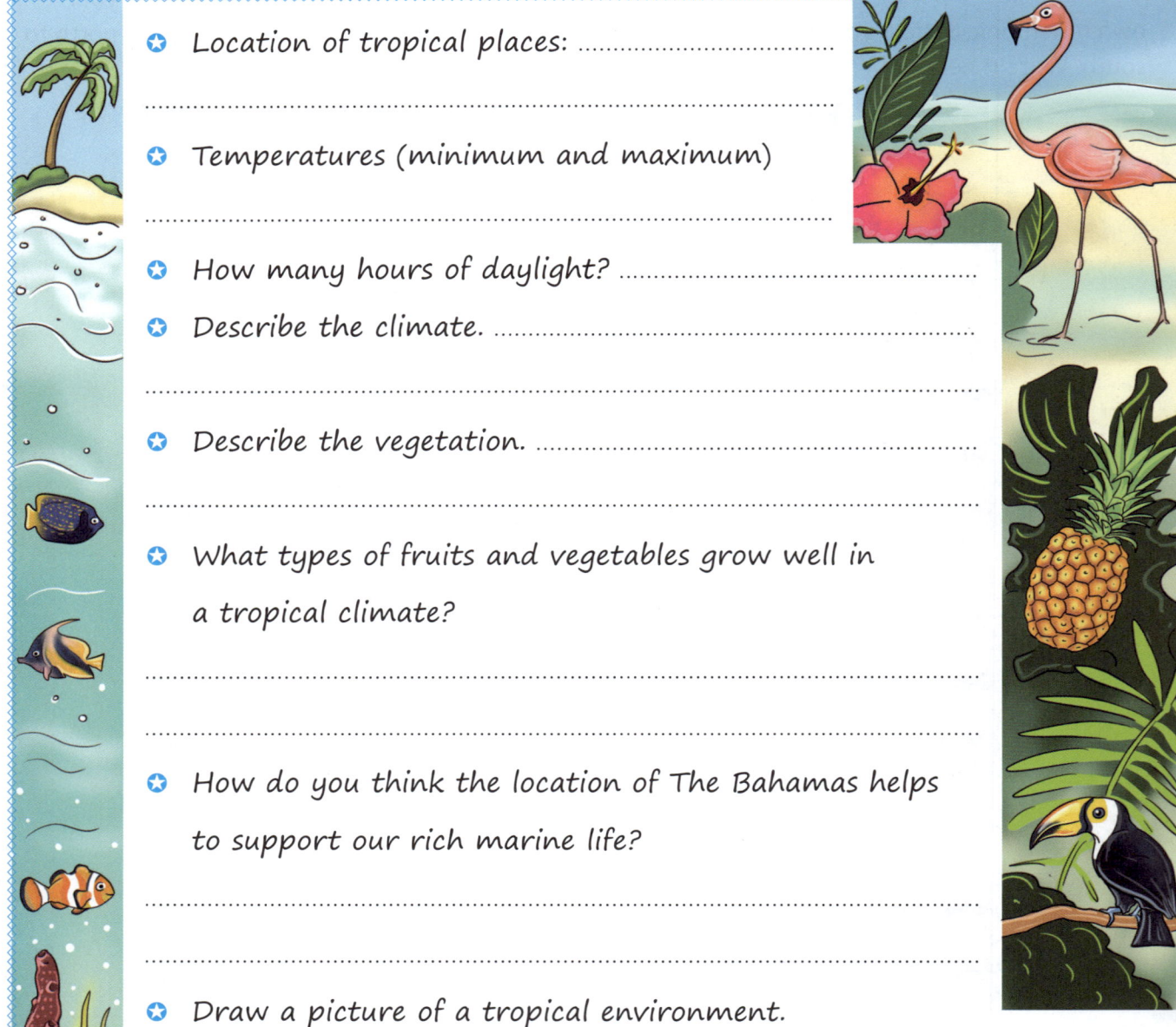

- Location of tropical places: ....
....

- Temperatures (minimum and maximum)
....

- How many hours of daylight? ....

- Describe the climate. ....
....

- Describe the vegetation. ....
....

- What types of fruits and vegetables grow well in a tropical climate?
....
....

- How do you think the location of The Bahamas helps to support our rich marine life?
....
....

- Draw a picture of a tropical environment.

The importance of the ocean banks

The ocean banks are a vital resource for The Bahamas. Tourists from all over the world come to visit our beaches and enjoy the rich marine life of our barrier reef. This provides income for many Bahamians who work in the tourist industry.

Design a tourist brochure that describes activities that visitors can enjoy in the Little Bahama Bank and Great Bahama Bank.

Chapter 2 Geography

Comparing our southern and northern islands

These graphs compare the climate on two different islands in The Bahamas.

Rainfall and temperature in Crooked Island and East Grand Bahama in one year

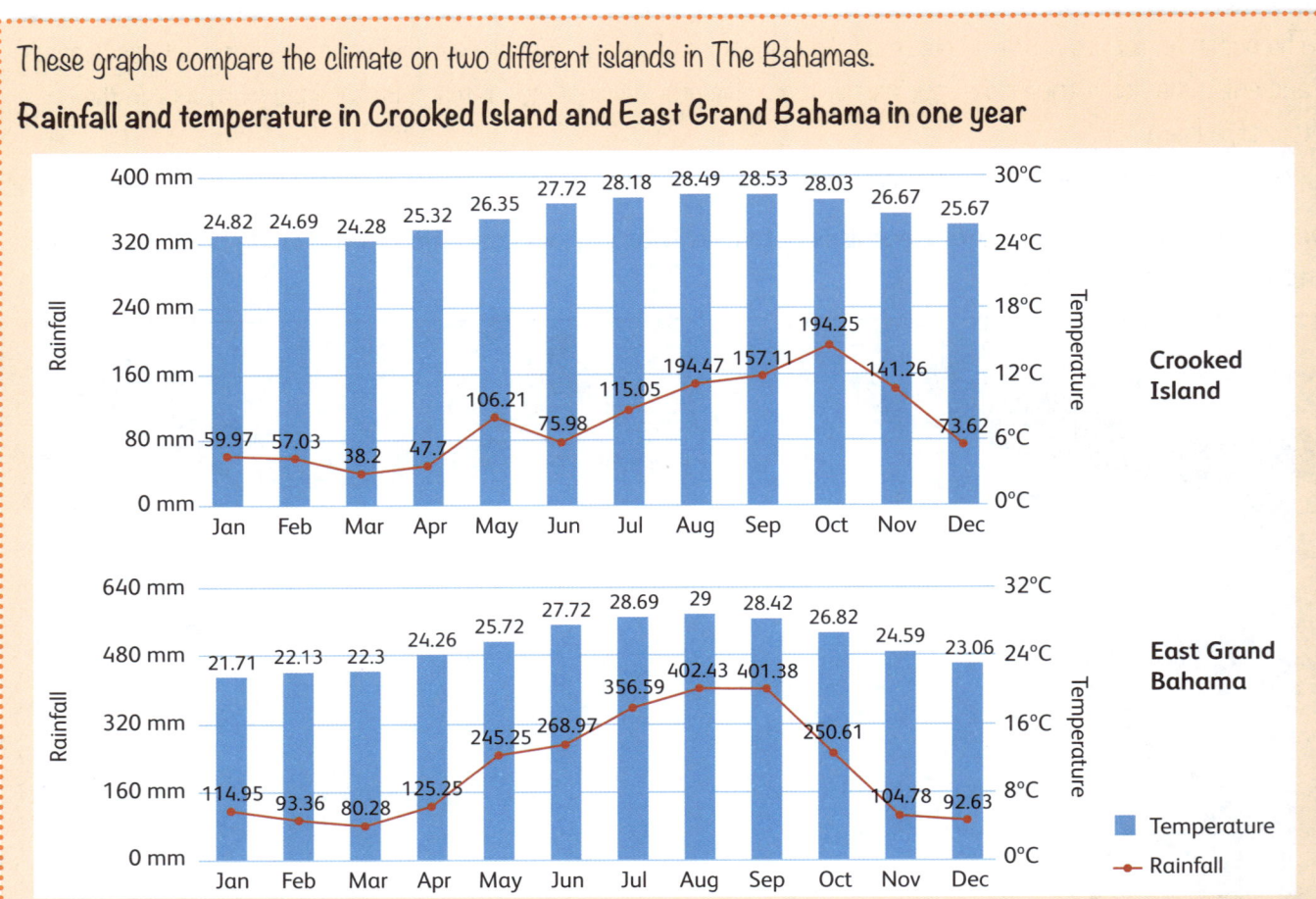

1. What similarity do you notice about the rainfall on these two islands?
   _____

2. Work with a partner. List some similarities and differences between the southern islands and other islands in The Bahamas.

   a   Geographic location:
   _____
   _____

   b   Climate:
   _____
   _____

   c   Population:
   _____
   _____

6 Natural resources

CHAPTER 3: Economics and resources

Resources are things that we use to meet our needs. **Natural** resources come from nature. What do you use every day that uses or comes from natural resources? For example, a kite, a windmill or a balloon uses air. What else can you think of that requires each of the natural resources below?

HINT
Think of the things you use, buy, wear and eat, or things people grow, use to build houses and make products. There are some words in each box to help you.

Air
wind • fresh air

Sunlight
heat • light • sunshine 

Water

Soil
seas • oceans • lakes • dams

trees • earth • rock • stones

Plants
rice • cotton • fruit • trees • vegetables

Animals
cows • chickens • fish • goats

Chapter 3 Economics and resources

Using our natural resources

1 Fill in each space, using the drawing before it as a clue. You can check if your answers are correct by matching these to the items in the key in your textbook.

We use land in many ways. We use it to build _____ where people can live. At the _____, children can play. People travel on _____, and sometimes need _____ if they need to cross a _____.

People work in _____ and _____, and also produce goods in _____. On farms, we grow _____ and _____ so we have enough food for people to eat. Farms also provide land for _____.

Any community also needs space for a _____, where we bury our dead.

2 Tick (✔) which activities match the correct water sources. You can tick more than one.

	Sea	River	Water tank	Rain
Swimming				
Watering crops				
Water for washing				
Fishing				
Transport (ships and boats)				

Unit 6 Natural resources

Natural resources in The Bahamas

Rivers and seas; beaches, soil and sand; rocks and minerals; plants and animals; wind, sunshine and rain – these are all **natural resources**. Write the correct name of each natural resource below the matching picture.

- blue holes
- pine forest
- aragonite
- salt ponds
- fish
- beaches
- arable land (good for farming)
- mangroves
- sponges

Chapter 3 Economics and resources

Plants are a natural resource

1. Plants have many uses. Fill this worksheet with pictures of the many things we get from plants.
   You can cut out and paste pictures from newspapers or magazines.
   You can also print or draw pictures.

Unit 6 Natural resources

2 For each type of food, write the name of the animal from which we get it.

a    b    c

_____   _____   _____

d    e    f

_____   _____   _____

3 a Name one animal which is reared in your community. _____

b What are three products we get from this animal?

_____

_____

c Rearing animals for meat and by-products uses large areas of land and also a huge amount of water. The gases released by cows add to global warming. Many scientists, vegetarians and people concerned about the ethical use of animals say that we should find **alternatives** to rearing animals for meat. Suggest two alternatives.

HINT

An alternative is a different choice or option.

_____

_____

_____

_____

47

Chapter 3 Economics and resources

Harvesting natural resources

A farmer **harvests** ripe fruits and vegetables. **Harvesting** means collecting resources to get them ready for use. When we talk about harvesting other natural resources, we refer to many different processes.

1 Look at each picture. Describe which natural resource is being harvested, and how you think it might be used. What makes this form of harvesting sustainable (or not)?

a

b

c

48

Unit 6 Natural resources

d

e

f

49

Chapter 3 Economics and resources

Foods we produce

In the past, Bahamians farmed sisal and harvested sea sponges in order to earn income. Today, we farm and harvest many other products. We also produce and manufacture a wide range of food products, both to consume in The Bahamas and for export.

1. Which crops (fruits and vegetables) grow on your island?

2. What animal-based foods are farmed on your island?

Unit 6 Natural resources

3 Businesses use many different ingredients to manufacture food products. What are your favourite food products manufactured in The Bahamas?

_____
_____
_____
_____
_____
_____

4 In the space below, paste labels from some local Bahamian food products. Around each label, list the main products or ingredients it is made from and how this is harvested. For example, conch chowder is made from conch, which is fished from the sea.

Chapter 3 Economics and resources

Preserving food

When we grow or catch food, we may sell it fresh or **preserve** it. Preserving means processing food so that it will not spoil quickly. There are many different methods of preserving food, including salting, pickling, drying, freezing, bottling and canning.

1. This flow diagram shows all the stages in canning fish. Some of the steps are missing a label. Choose and fill in these labels below the correct steps.

   Labelling   Freezing   Thawing   Filling   Steam cooking   Sterilising

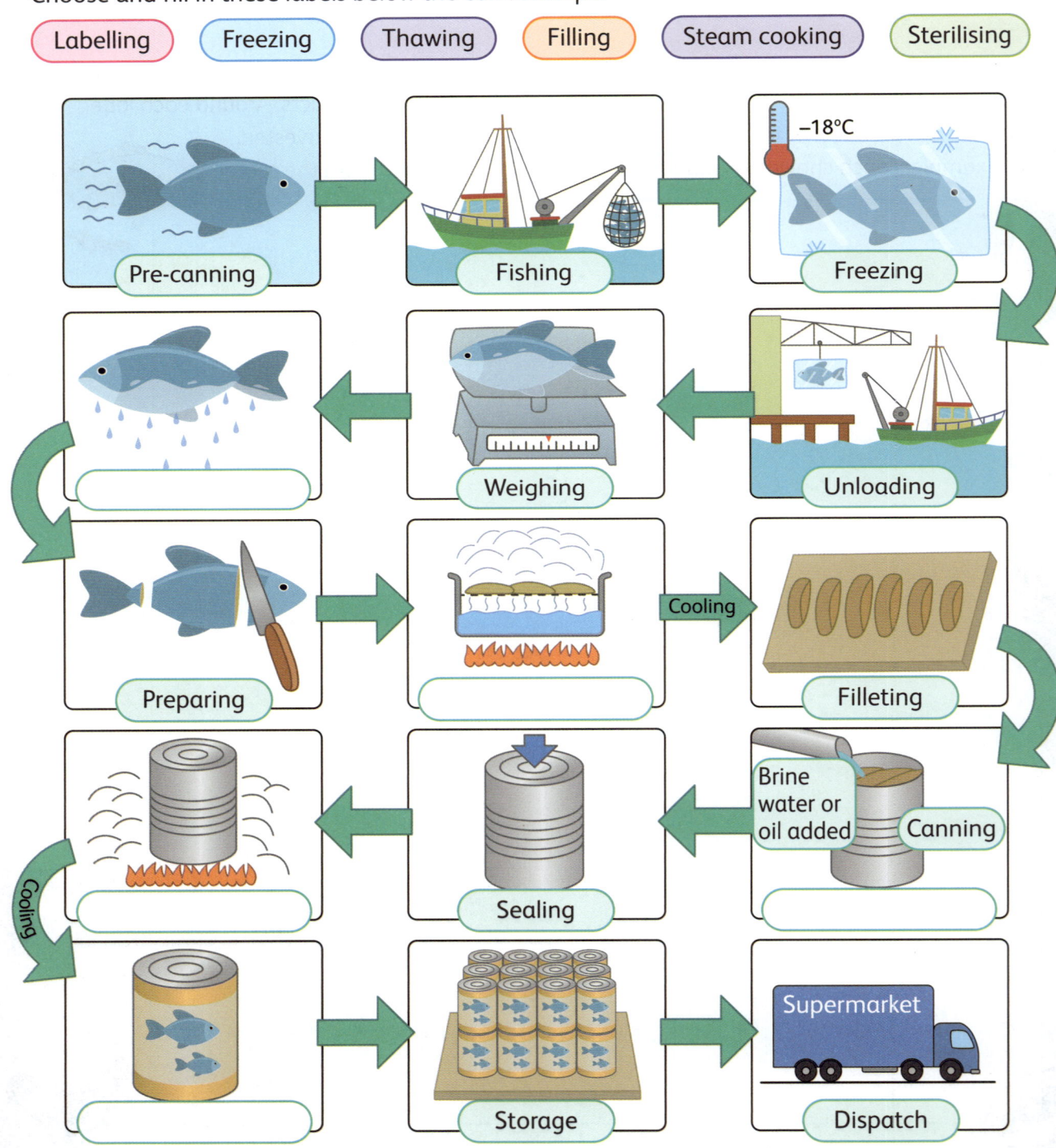

2 Choose three of the methods of preserving listed at the start of the previous page. For each method, write or draw foods that your family likes to eat which are preserved in this way.

Method: _____ **Examples:**

Method: _____ **Examples:**

Method: _____ **Examples:**

Chapter 3 Economics and resources

Jobs in food production

Food production is any business that makes products that we eat. There are many different jobs in food production. Some involve farming crops, raising livestock or catching wild sources of food. Others involve developing and manufacturing products. There are many jobs that deal with health, safety and food hygiene.

1. Think of five different food products that your family likes to eat regularly. Write them in the centre of each mind map. Then brainstorm three different jobs that people do in the production of each food, and complete the mindmaps.

2. Discuss ideas with your classmates. What other jobs in food production can you think of?

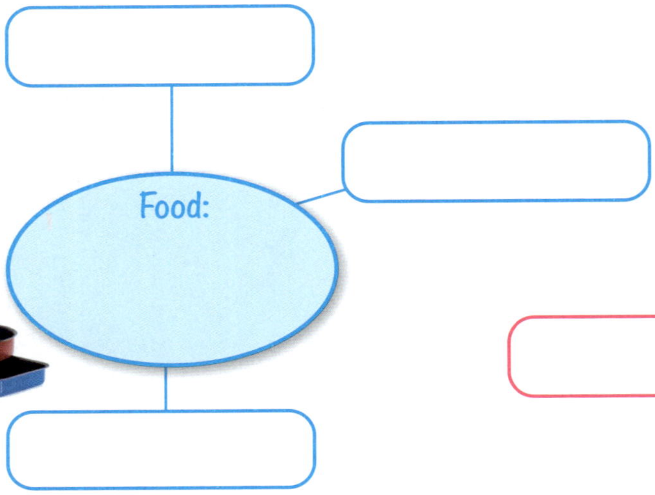

Food:

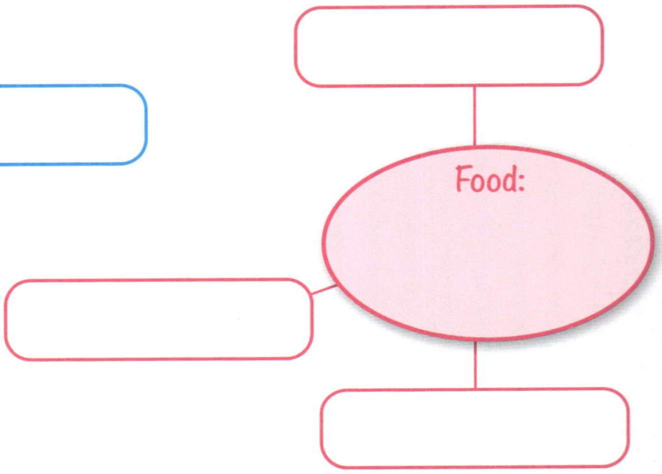

Food:

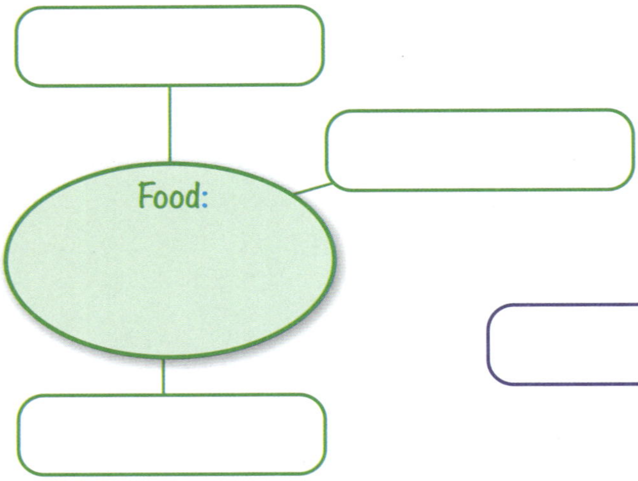

Food:

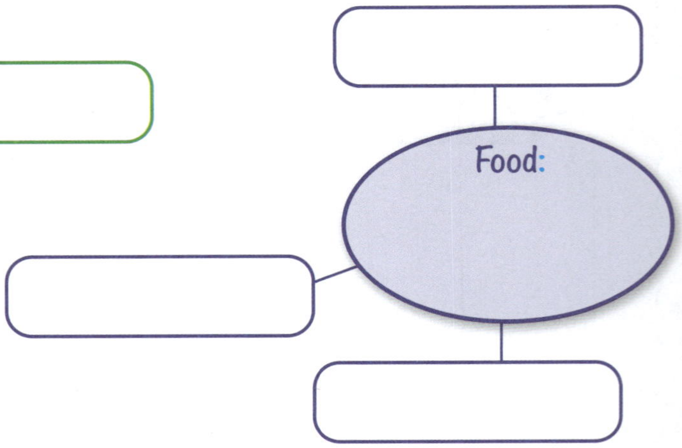

Food:

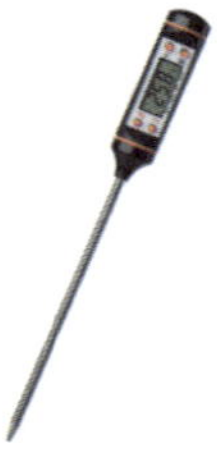

54

Unit 6 Natural resources

3 Choose a job from the food production industry that sounds interesting to you. Find out more about it. You can:
- find information on the internet
- visit a business where people do this job (you may need to call first and make a request)
- talk to people you know in your family and community.

Use this questionnaire to help you gather information.

JOB TITLE:

✪ Description of what the job involves:
....
....
....

✪ I find this job interesting because:
....
....
....

✪ Names of companies or businesses that offer this type of job:
....
....

✪ What kind of training do people need for this job?
....
....
....

✪ What could make the job difficult?
....
....
....

✪ Any other information:
....
....
....

Chapter 3 Economics and resources

Resources create jobs

Have a class discussion about the natural resources of The Bahamas, and how these resources create jobs. Then complete this multiple-choice quiz to check your knowledge!

1. Why do only some crops grow well in The Bahamas?
    a There is not enough space to grow many crops.
    b Our climate and soil are only suitable for certain crops.
    c There is a shortage of farming equipment.

2. Cascarilla, aragonite and salt are examples of:
    a crops that grow well in The Bahamas
    b materials used in the fishing industry
    c raw materials that are shipped abroad and earn additional income for The Bahamas.

3. Bahamian produce is collected in packing houses, and then shipped to distribution points on the island of:
    a New Providence
    b Mayaguana
    c San Salvador.

4. In the past, the main natural resources used for earning money were:
    a fish and salt
    b sisal and sponge
    c platinum and coral.

5. Examples of preserving processes for food items include:
    a ploughing, sowing and harvesting
    b producing, manufacturing and
    c canning, bottling, freezing and drying.

7 Tourism in The Bahamas

The tourist industry

One of the biggest industries in the Caribbean is tourism. Tourists are people who visit a country. There are many kinds of tourism:

* **leisure tourism** – people who visit a country for holidays and fun
* **business tourism** – people who visit for conferences or work reasons
* **medical tourism** – people who visit to get healthcare that they cannot get in their own country, or that they prefer to get in another country.

Caribbean visitors are people who travel from their home country in the Caribbean to other Caribbean countries. Non-Caribbean visitors come from other countries.

1. Visit a tourism office or contact your local tourism authority to do some research about tourism in The Bahamas. If possible, find out how many tourists entered the country in:

    a   2018   b   2019   c   2020

    _____
    _____

2. Why do you think visitor numbers went down in 2020?
    _____
    _____

3. If possible, find out the following figures for the last calendar year:

    a   How many Caribbean visitors entered the country? _____
    b   How many non-Caribbean visitors entered the country? _____

4. a   Were there more Caribbean or non-Caribbean visitors?
    _____
    _____

    b   Why do you think this was the case?
    _____
    _____

Chapter 3 Economics and resources

How does tourism benefit The Bahamas?

1. With a partner, brainstorm the ways that tourism benefits The Bahamas. Draw a mind map with your ideas below. Use these words to help you.

   infrastructure · development · transport · jobs · culture · preserve
   national pride · education · environment · opportunity · exchange

2. The Covid-19 pandemic made tourism very difficult. What impact do you think this had on The Bahamas? Discuss it with your family and share your ideas here.

Unit 7 Tourism in The Bahamas

Family members employed in tourism

Do a class survey to find out how many students' family members are employed in tourism, compared to other industries.

1. Do a tally chart. Draw a tally for each family member employed in each industry.

Industry	Number of family members
Fishing	
Farming	
Food production	
Tourism	
Finance	
Other	

2. The total number of family members represented in the tally chart is _____

3. Write the fraction of the total employed in each industry.

Fishing	Farming	Food production	Tourism	Finance	Other

4. Use your information to draw a pie chart.

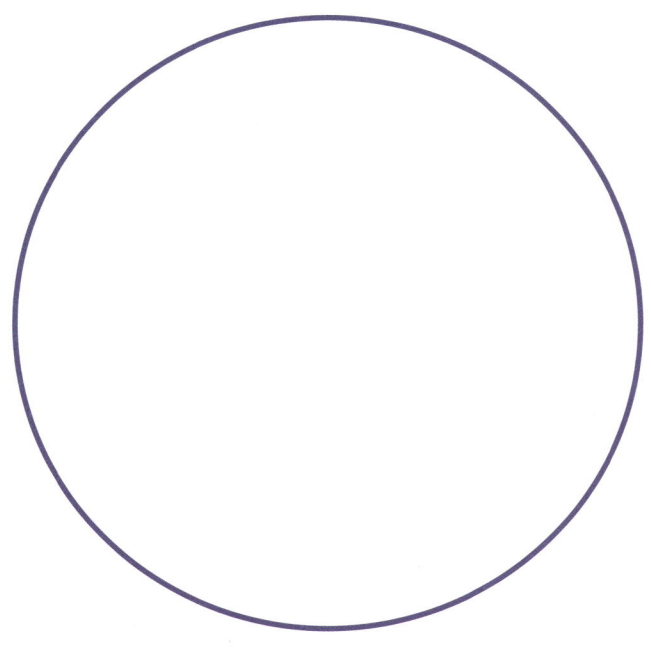

HINT

You will need to express each fraction out of 360 in order to work out the angles in the pie chart.

Chapter 3 Economics and resources

Tourist attractions

A **tourist attraction** is a place that attracts tourists to visit. It may be a place of natural beauty, such as a beach, a forest or a lookout point. It may be a natural feature such as a volcano, waterfall or mountain path. Some tourist attractions are places of cultural interest such as great houses, museums, churches, cultural centres or local markets. Others involve activities such as snorkeling, scuba diving, hiking or fishing.

List the top four tourist destinations that tourists like to visit in your country. Draw or glue a picture and write a short description.

Sir Stafford Sands

Use the internet or your textbook to find out more about Sir Stafford Lofthouse Sands. Complete this ⭐fact file.

- ⭐ Date of birth: ....
- ⭐ Mother's name: ....
  ....
- ⭐ Father's name: ....
  ....
- ⭐ He died on: ....
- ⭐ Which important position did he hold from 1964 to 1967? ....
  ....
- ⭐ Other important positions he held:
  ....
  ....
  ....
  ....
  ....

- ⭐ Sir Stafford Sands introduced air conditioning, increased tax incentives and improvements in air transportation in the early 1960s. Why do you think this earned him the title of 'the Father of Tourism'?
  ....
  ....
  ....
  ....

- ⭐ Where does his portrait appear in everyday life in The Bahamas?
  ....
  ....

Sir Stafford Sands

Chapter 3 Economics and resources

A tourism timeline

Read the information about the development of tourism in The Bahamas. Choose key events from this history, and use them to create a timeline on pages 64–65.

The tourism industry of Bahamas has its roots in the 1850s, when the Government passed several acts to encourage tourism. The first **Tourism Encouragement Act** was passed in 1851, a second was passed in 1854, and the third in 1857 granted the Government authority to buy land to build **a grand hotel**.

Two years later, the Government agreed to pay the Cunard Line £3000 per year for a regular **steamship** service to the islands.

In 1898, new laws were passed to promote tourism to The Bahamas. The Hotel Colonial in Fort Nassau opened in 1900. The owner, Henry Flagler, also set up his own steamship service between Florida and Nassau.

The Cunard Line was the world's most well-known steamship company

The **Tourism Development Board** was established in 1914, with the aim of promoting The Bahamas. In 1919, the first seaplane service began between Florida and The Bahamas.

By 1929, Pan American airlines added a daily air service. Tourism flourished in the 1920s, with new hotels being built. The era of **prohibition** in the US drove many visitors to The Bahamas to buy rum. However, tourism slowed down in the 1930s because of the **Great Depression**.

An early Pan American Airways seaplane from about 1930

Unit 7 Tourism in The Bahamas

Up until the 1940s, the Bahamian tourism industry had enjoyed short bursts of growth, and then slumps. Tourists typically only visited when they wanted to escape winter in the northern hemisphere, between November and February. The government decided to establish a more stable, year-round industry. In 1950, Sir Stafford Sands gave the Tourism Development Board a budget of $500,000. Many new hotels were built in the 1950s.

The Hawksbill Creek Agreement of 1946 committed the Grand Bahama Port Authority to create a port and industrial area on 50,000 acres of land. The port was built in the 1950s, but instead of an industrial area, Grand Bahama developed large hotels and casinos.

In 1961, after Fidel Castro led a **coup in Cuba**, America imposed a trade embargo on Cuba. Cuba had been a popular tourist destination, but now American tourists turned to The Bahamas as an alternative. By 1968, for the first time The Bahamas had 1 million visitors in a single year.

The tourism industry has suffered many **setbacks** since the 1970s. When The Bahamas gained independence in 1973, many investors pulled out. Many Bahamians felt that tourism, a service industry, was built on the same principle of servitude that characterised their status as a colony. At the same time, the world was facing an **oil crisis**, as the price of oil rose dramatically, which led to fewer visitors. Between 1969 and 1979, a new program was put in place to improve tourism. It included staff training, marketing campaigns and new tourist initiatives and activities for hotels to offer visitors. In the 1980s, the popularity of cruise ships brought hundreds of thousands of visitors. However, many of these visitors only stop in The Bahamas for the day. The 1980s also brought more competition as other Caribbean countries became popular, particularly Jamaica, Puerto Rico and Aruba. The Gulf War in 1991, and later the damage from Hurricane Floyd in 1999, were also serious blows to tourism.

Despite many setbacks, tourism is one of the biggest industries in The Bahamas. Many people make their living from this vital industry.

Resort hotels in The Bahamas

Chapter 3 Economics and resources

Tourism timeline

Draw your own timeline of the development of tourism in The Bahamas. You can use information from the previous pages, as well as your own research. If you wish, you may choose a specific time period (for example the 1800s, 1900s or 20th century).

Unit 7 Tourism in The Bahamas

A tourism brochure from the past

Imagine that you were employed by the Tourism Development Board in the 1930s. One of your tasks is to design a brochure promoting tourism. Write a brochure intended to attract visitors to The Bahamas. Think about what attractions the island offered, the type of transport and accommodation. Try to use the style of language and images that people liked at that time!

Unit 7 Tourism in The Bahamas

Tips for how to treat tourists

As part of your job with the Tourism Development Board, you need to write guidelines for people who work in the tourist industry, such as hotel staff, drivers and tour guides. Write a list of ten tips for providing outstanding service to visitors. If possible, watch commercials or videos on this topic, or discuss it with your classmates or family.

#	
1	
2	
3	
4	
5	
6	
7	
8	
9	
10	

Chapter 3 Economics and resources

The different types of tourists

> The Bahamas receives different types of tourists – domestic, international, stopover, cruise ship passengers, and day visitors.

1. Discuss with a partner which type of tourist each example best describes. Tick the correct column or columns.

   1 – Domestic   2 – International   3 – Stopover   4 – Cruise ship   5 – Day visitor

Example or description	1	2	3	4	5
Someone who travels to countries outside of the country where they usually live					
Someone who takes holidays in different towns within their home country					
Someone who travels as a passenger on a cruise liner					
Someone who spends less than 24 hours visiting a place					
Someone who stays longer than 24 hours					
Ben works in Freeport, and flies to Miami for a week for a conference.					
Shana lives in New Providence and goes to visit family in Nicholl's Town for three days.					
Luis lives in Portugal and takes a two-week cruise to the Caribbean, spending one day in Bimini and one day in Nassau.					

2. Write three of your own examples of tourists that match the ticked columns.

Example or description	1	2	3	4	5
	✔				✔
		✔		✔	
	✔		✔		

68

Market research about tourism

> When we do **market research**, we find out about what kinds of new services or products would be suitable for a market. We can ask people questions to find out about their knowledge and opinions about a particular product or service.

Interview an adult in your family or community about tourism in The Bahamas.

1. Where in The Bahamas do you live? ....

2. a What work do you do? ....
   b Is this work directly or indirectly involved with tourism? If yes, give details.
   ....
   ....

3. Which places do tourists like to visit on your island?
   ....
   ....

4. Rate how strongly you agree or disagree with each statement.

   1 – Strongly agree
   2 – Slightly agree
   3 – Do not have an opinion
   4 – Slightly disagree
   5 – Strongly disagree

   a Tourism is an important industry in The Bahamas. ☐
   b Other industries are more important for The Bahamas. ☐
   c I would like to see more visitors in The Bahamas. ☐
   d I feel my island gets enough tourist visitors. ☐
   e I travel to other countries at least once per year. ☐
   f I travel regularly within The Bahamas. ☐
   g It is easy to reach my island from the other main islands in The Bahamas. ☐

Chapter 3 Economics and resources

5 Do you feel there is opportunity for more tourist services on your island? Tick any of the following.

Hotels ☐
Resorts ☐
Bus or taxi services ☐
Cafés and restaurants ☐
Ecotourism ☐
Shops catering for tourists ☐
Entertainment ☐
Guided tours ☐
Ecotourism ☐
Online information for visitors ☐
Cultural sites ☐
Historical sites ☐
Other ☐

If you ticked 'Other', give some suggestions or ideas.

....
....
....

2 When you have completed your research, discuss with your classmates the information they collected. Use it to to suggest two ways for catering better for tourism on your island.

8 Transport and communication

Forms of transportation

Think about the different forms of transportation people use in The Bahamas. Write, draw or glue examples of each type of transportation into the table.

	Private	Public
By sea		
By land		
By air		

Chapter 3 Economics and resources

Transportation stations

Airports, bus stop, cruise ship ports and harbours are all examples of **transportation stations**.

If possible, visit a transportation station. Complete the ⭐fact file about your visit.

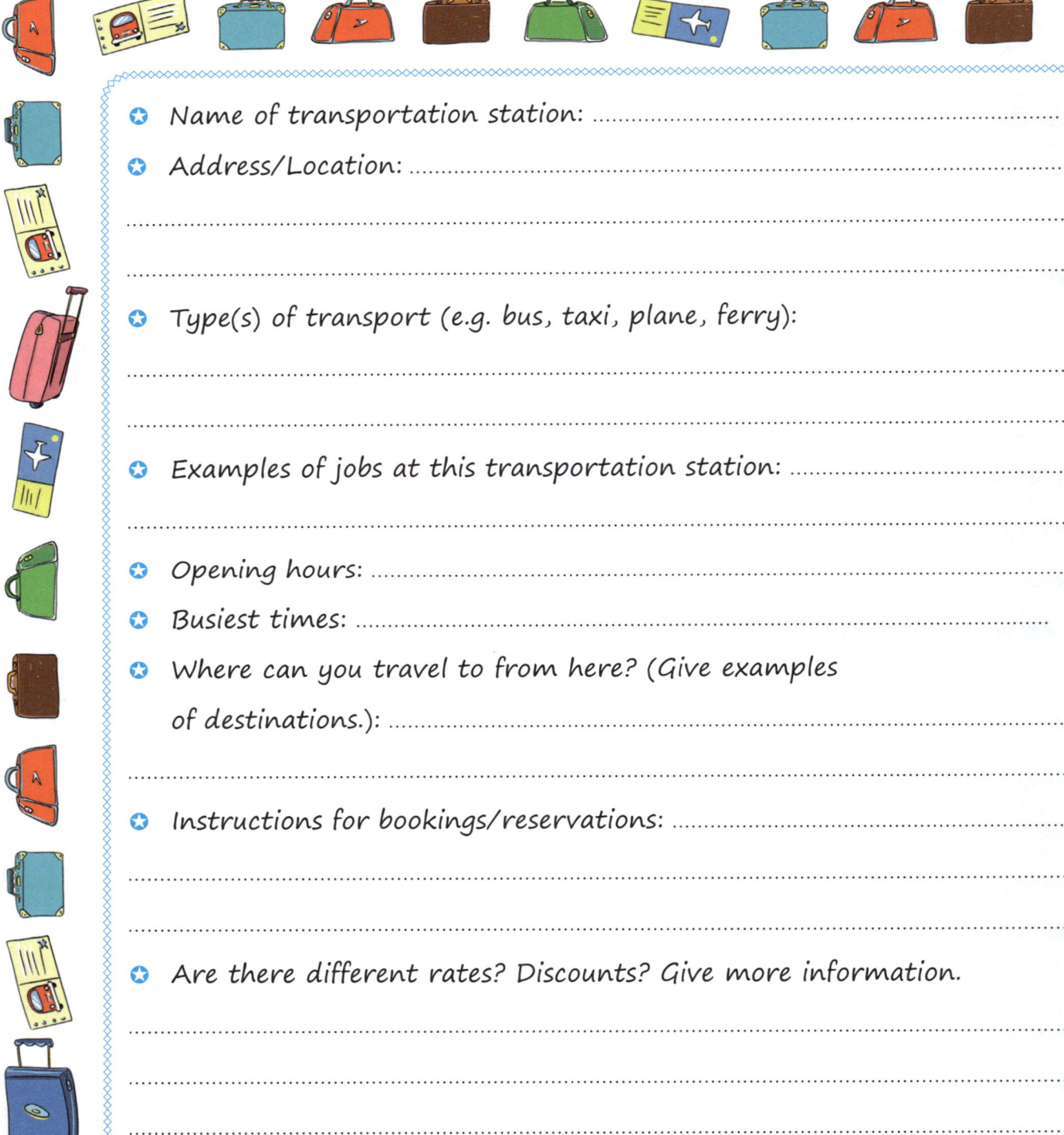

- Name of transportation station: ....
- Address/Location: ....

  ....

- Type(s) of transport (e.g. bus, taxi, plane, ferry):

  ....

- Examples of jobs at this transportation station: ....

  ....

- Opening hours: ....
- Busiest times: ....
- Where can you travel to from here? (Give examples of destinations.): ....

  ....

- Instructions for bookings/reservations: ....

  ....

- Are there different rates? Discounts? Give more information.

  ....

  ....

Unit 8 Transport and communication

- Can customers find information online? If so, give the web address.

....

....

- If offline booking is possible, give brief booking/reservation instructions.

....

....

....

- Are there other facilities available at the transportation station, for example restaurants, restrooms, lockers, information services? Give details.

....

....

....

....

- Draw or paste in a picture of the transportation station.

73

Chapter 3 Economics and resources

Benefits of international transportation

International visitors to The Bahamas arrive by sea or by air from all over the world. Cruise ships, cargo ships, yachts and other boats all arrive by sea. Most are commercial vessels, but some are privately owned. Similarly, most planes that fly into The Bahamas are commercial airline planes, but there are also private planes that use the airports.

1. If possible, visit a dock, marina or airport. Make notes about the ships or planes that you see. Try to work out where they come from.

Description of plane or ship – Airline/Shipping line/Name	Country of origin	Likely reason for arrival – cargo, passengers, business, holidaymakers

2. This graph shows the origin of stopover tourists in 2016.

    a Why do you think such a large proportion of our tourists come from the USA?

    _____

    _____

    _____

    b List three benefits of international transportation to The Bahamas.

    _____

    _____

    _____

    _____

    _____

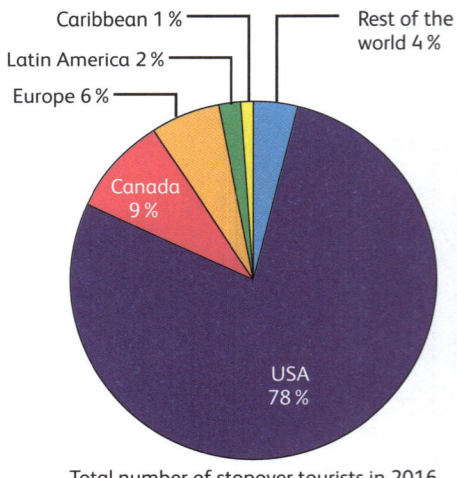

Total number of stopover tourists in 2016
1,500,000

Technological advances in communication and transport

Communication is the sending and receiving of **messages** from one individual or group to another. For thousands of years, humans have communicated using gestures, words and written symbols. **Telecommunication** is the term we use to describe communication over a distance, for example by telephone or the internet. Some forms of telecommunication are sent from one sender to one receiver. Others are **broadcast** to millions of people at the same time.

1876	1926	1946	1973	1992	2001 to present
The first telephone used landline technology. The sound travelled along wires.	The first transatlantic call was placed from London to New York.	Area codes allowed people to call directly from one location to another.	The first mobile phone was a large brick-shaped device, the first telephone that did not require wires.	The first SMS (short message service) was sent from one mobile to another.	Increasing improvements in wireless technology and internet service (internet, WiFi, smartphones, apps, cloud computing and more).

1. Describe a form of modern communication that you would use to:
   a find out about weather conditions in another country _____
   b book a flight to another island _____
   c speak to a relative in the next village _____
   d listen to the news while in a car _____
   e listen to music while on a bus _____

2. In 1876, the telephone was the newest technology. Explain three ways in which this technology was improved later in the 1900s.

3. Name three new technologies that were developed after 2001. For each one, say how it benefited the way we could communicate.

Chapter 3 Economics and resources

Using a GPS

Until recently, a drivers would keep a local mapbook or roadmap in their car so that they could find any address. Today, most people no longer use these types of map. Instead we use GPS (Global Positioning System) or Satnav (satellite navigation) systems to find our way to any address. This is possible because of new technologies.

A satellite navigation system in a car

1. a GPS stands for _____

   b Satnav comes from the words _____

2. Brainstorm the advantages and disadvantages of each way of finding your way around.

	Advantages	Disadvantages
Printed road maps		
Navigation systems or GPS		

3. Work with a partner or family member. Use an app (such as Google Maps) or satellite navigation system to work out a route to a place in your town or village. Follow the directions to your destination.

   a Was it easy or difficult to follow the directions? Give reasons.

   _____

   _____

   b Which information did the app provide?

   Time to destination ☐   Distance to destination ☐   Places of interest ☐

   Map ☐   Map scale ☐   North pointer ☐

   Other: _____

   c What safety guidelines would you give someone for using a navigation system on a phone?

   _____

   _____

   _____

The uses of weather apps

For thousands of years, human beings have tried to predict the weather. Modern technologies allow us to do this more accurately than ever before, and communication technologies help us to share and find this information instantly.

1 Brainstorm ways that information about the weather can be helpful. Add your own ideas around each of the headings in the mind map below.

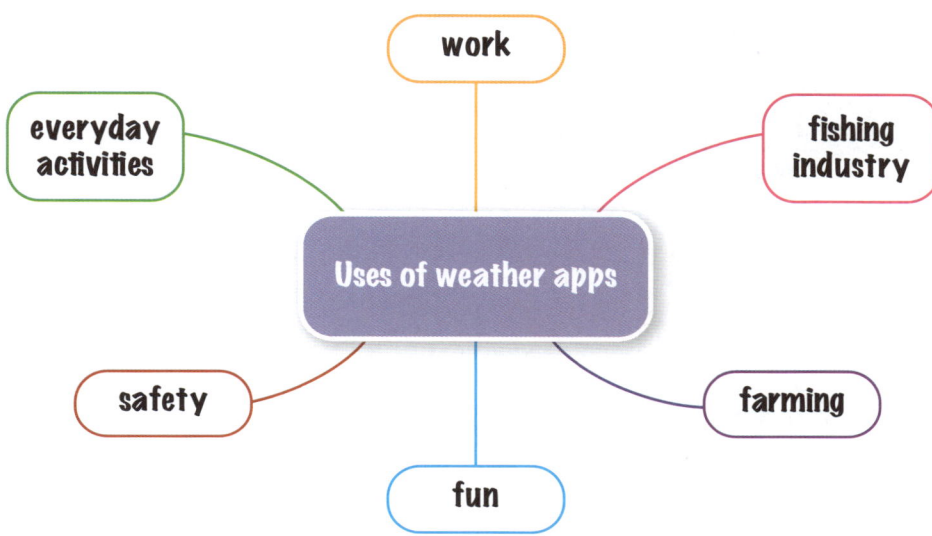

2 Use a smartphone or computer. Open an app or website with weather information. What information did you find?

- Date: ....
- Weather conditions: ....
- Temperature: ....
- Humidity: ....
- Rain: ....
- Wind speed: ....
- Forecast for the coming days: ....
  ....
  ....

77

9 Farming and fishing

Farming in The Bahamas

> All people need food to live. **Farming** means cultivating the land to grow crops for food, or raising livestock. Livestock are farmed animals such as **poultry** (chicken) and **cattle** (animals such as goats, sheep, pigs and cows), which provide meat and milk.

❶ Explain how each of these natural resources helps Bahamians to provide food or income.

a
large flat areas of land

b
sunshine all year round

c
large area of sea around our islands

❷ List at least five examples each of field crops, vegetables and fruits.

Field crops	Vegetables	Fruits

Unit 9 Farming and fishing

Where our produce comes from

> We grow some of our own produce **locally** in The Bahamas, but we also **import** many products. Imported produce tends to be more expensive because of the cost of transporting it from other countries.

1. Visit a supermarket or grocery store. Look at the labels on a variety of fruits and vegetables.

   a List them in this table.

Imported produce			Local produce	
Type of fruit/vegetable	Country of origin	Price	Type of fruit/vegetable	Price

   b Where do most of our important fruits and vegetables come from? _____

   c Which other countries do we import from? _____

   d Do you agree with the statement that imported produce is more expensive? What does your research show? _____

   e What other disadvantages are there about importing produce? _____

2. Use an atlas to help you answer the first two questions.

   a Name the two main islands in The Bahamas for poultry farming.

   b Name the three main fishing grounds in The Bahamas.

   c Name three products that we produce from cow milk.

   d Farming also produces materials that we use to make other products. Think of at least two farmed materials that we use to make clothing or other materials.

79

CHAPTER 4: Government

10 Our leaders

All groups need leaders

1. All citizens have a responsibility to love, cherish, develop and defend our nation. Give an example of how we can demonstrate this in everyday ways.

2. What do you understand by the term 'role model'?

3. Name role models in your community, and explain what you admire about them.

Unit 10 Our leaders

4. Complete this ⭐fact file about the way your country is governed.

My country

- Form of government (pick one):

  constitutional monarchy   constitutional republic

  parliamentary republic

- Which voting procedure best describes the country?
  - [ ] simple majority – first past the post
  - [ ] two-round system
  - [ ] proportional representation
  - [ ] other

- The leader of the country, or head of state, is known as the
  ....

- The head of the government is known as
  ....

- Describe the main functions of these leaders.

- Who is allowed to vote in the country's general elections?
  ....

- Why is voting an important responsibility?
  ....

81

Our Governors-General and Prime Ministers

Complete the names of our Governors-General and Prime Ministers since independence.

Our Governors-General

Sir John _____ Paul

Sir Milo _____ Butler (first Bahamian Governor-General)

Sir Gerald _____

Sir Henry _____ Taylor

Sir Clifford _____

Sir Orville _____

Dame Ivy _____ (first woman Governor-General of The Bahamas)

The Hon. Paul L. _____

The Hon. Arthur Dion _____

Sir Arthur _____

Dame Marguerite _____

Sir Cornelius A. _____ _____

Our Prime Ministers

Rt. Hon. Sir Lynden Oscar _____

Rt. Hon. Hubert _____ _____

Rt. Hon. Perry _____ _____

Most Rt. Hon. Hubert _____ _____

Rt. Hon. Philip _____ _____

Unit 10 Our leaders

Write a mnemonic

Write a **mnemonic** to help you remember the names of all our Governors-General and Prime Ministers in the correct order.

HINT
A mnemonic is an acrostic, poem, rhyme or song that helps you to remember a set of words in order.

Our Governors-General

Our Prime Ministers

Chapter 4 Government

If I were Governor-General

1. Explain what you think the main role of the Governor-General is.

   _____
   _____
   _____

2. Imagine that you were Governor-General. What specific goals would you like to achieve for The Bahamas in this position? Write three goals here.

   _____
   _____
   _____
   _____
   _____
   _____

3. Imagine a day in the life of the Governor-General. Write what you think a typical day would involve.

   _____
   _____
   _____
   _____
   _____
   _____
   _____
   _____
   _____
   _____
   _____
   _____

Unit 10 Our leaders

4. Draw a picture to show one of the things that you think the Governor-General would be doing on a typical day. Add a descriptive heading.

Chapter 4 Government

The Prime Minister

In The Bahamas, the head of the Government is the Prime Minister. The two main political parties in The Bahamas are the Progressive Liberal Party and the Free National Movement.

1. Imagine you are writing a job advertisement for people who want to apply to become Prime Minister. Write the job description and the main skills required.

> **WANTED! Future Prime Minister ...
> do you have what it takes?**
> ....
> ....
> ....
> ....
> ....

2. Think about what it would be like to the Prime Minister. List pros (positive aspects, or things you would like) and cons (negative aspects, or things you would not like) about the job.

Pros	Cons

3. If you were a Member of Parliament, which issue would be your highest priority? Give details here, and explain why you think it is important.

_____
_____
_____
_____

4. Name the current Minister of Youth, Sports and Culture, and explain why you think this is an important role. _____
_____

11 Rights and responsibilities

Moral standards

Our **moral standards** are our beliefs about what is right and what is wrong. Our morals guide our behaviour and our actions. For example, trustworthiness is widely accepted as a good moral standard. This would guide our actions:

Morally acceptable
- ✔ speaking the truth
- ✔ keeping promises
- ✔ honouring commitments

Morally unacceptable
- ✘ lying
- ✘ breaking trust

Work with a partner. Brainstorm behaviours that you find morally acceptable and unacceptable, based on the values below.

Morally acceptable / Respect / Morally unacceptable

Morally acceptable / Responsibility / Morally unacceptable

Morally acceptable / Caring / Morally unacceptable

Morally acceptable / Fairness / Morally unacceptable

87

Chapter 4 Government

Moral behaviour

1. With a partner, brainstorm things you can do at school and in the community that would demonstrate your commitment to the values you explored on page 50.

At school

In my community

2. Exemplary conduct means the best possible behaviour. Think of someone at school whose behaviour demonstrates excellent moral standards.

   a Describe what kind of behaviour you would describe as exemplary.

   b Suggest a way we could recognise exemplary conduct.

   c Suggest ways to encourage more children to behave in this way.

3. Some types of behaviour are not wrong morally but may be frowned upon at school. Write three things you can do at home but not at school.

Unit 11 Rights and responsibilities

Differences of opinion

Sometimes, people may hold differing views about what is morally acceptable and what is morally unacceptable.

1 Read the different statements. Choose one, and write your own views about it.

> My sister is a vegetarian. She says it is morally unacceptable to kill animals and eat meat. But I disagree, as long as the animals are kept in humane conditions.

> I know it is unacceptable to lie. But sometimes, telling the truth can hurt people's feelings.

> Sometimes I promise to do something, but then circumstances change and it is not possible to keep my promise. What is the right thing to do?

_____
_____
_____
_____
_____
_____
_____
_____

2 Describe another situation where people might agree on what is morally acceptable.

_____
_____
_____
_____
_____

Chapter 4 Government

Taking personal and group responsibility

1. As a class, brainstorm the ways that you can take responsibility for moral behaviour as an individual and as a group.

   a   Ways I can take responsibility for my own moral behaviour:

   _____
   _____
   _____
   _____

   b   Ways that we can take responsibility for our behaviour as a group:

   _____
   _____
   _____
   _____

2. Draw up your own declaration of moral responsibility. Write it here and sign it.

   _____
   _____
   _____
   _____
   _____
   _____
   _____

3. What does it mean to have a 'Caribbean identity'? What do people from different countries in the Caribbean have in common? What do we take responsibility for as part of a regional group? Write your own ideas.

   _____
   _____
   _____
   _____

The Universal Declaration of Human Rights

All human beings are entitled to **human rights** and these rights are protected by laws. For example, everyone has the right to live freely without fear of violence. The **Universal Declaration of Human Rights** (UDHR) is a statement that was adopted in 1948 at a General Assembly of the United Nations (UN).

1. Find the full text of the UDHR at https://www.un.org/en/universal-declaration-human-rights/. Use the Declaration to help you to decide whether each statement is true or false. After each statement is a clue about which Article to read. If it is false, correct the statement.

   a You have the right to freedom from prejudice, bias or stereotyping based on your race, gender, nationality or religion. **(Article 2)**

   b Some people have the right to be free from slavery. **(Article 4)**

   c Your government may arrest or imprison you for any reason. **(Article 9)**

   d Consenting adults have the right to marry and raise a family. **(Article 16)**

   e Parents may decide not to educate their children if they do not wish to. **(Article 26)**

   f No country, group or person may use this declaration to deny the rights or freedoms of others. **(Article 30)**

2. Choose any other Article from the Declaration. Explain what it says and why you believe it is important.

Rights and freedoms in our Constitution

Each country has its own particular way of stating the rights and freedoms of its citizens. You can find these in the country's **Constitution**. A Constitution is a **legal document**, and it may be very long, with very **formal language**. The statements are known as **provisions** or **clauses**, and they are usually numbered, sometimes with letters for each sub-clause. Here are some tips for finding the rights and freedoms within the Constitution of The Bahamas.

* Find the Contents section. Is there a particular section or chapter that deals with rights and freedoms? Look for these key words: **fundamental human rights, rights enshrined, freedoms**.

* Go to the section that deals with these rights. Some Constitutions will have notes alongside the main text, indicating the topic of each article or provision. Use these to help you.

Research the Constitution of The Bahamas. Your school may have a printed copy, or you may be able to find it on the internet.

1. What is the title and date of our country's Constitution?

2. Quote the provision or clause from the Constitution that shows how The Bahamas protects each of the following basic human rights. Add a note of any responsibilities which are tied to each right (for example, freedom of speech includes the responsibility not to say things which discriminate against others or are illegal):

   a freedom to act according to one's own conscience

   b freedom to meet and gather peacefully in groups (freedom of assembly)

   c freedom of movement and travel: what responsibilities are tied to this right?

   d freedom of speech: what responsibilities are tied to this right?

Human rights violations

> **Human rights violations** are situations where people are denied their rights or freedoms. They are also called **human rights abuses**. Even though most countries agree in principle to the universal rights of their citizens, violations do still take place.

❶ Read each speech bubble. Identify which human rights are being violated in each situation.

I come from a very poor country. My family home does not have electricity or running water, because the government says they do not have enough money to provide for everyone.

In my country, the government is very corrupt. My father was part of an opposition party and was speaking out against the government. One night, some police arrived in an unmarked vehicle and arrested him. We are worried for his safety.

I work in a factory. The hours are very long, and the pay is very low. In order to earn enough for my family, I need to work as many hours as I can. I hardly get any time to rest. I worry that if I get ill, nobody will provide for us.

_____   _____   _____
_____   _____   _____
_____   _____   _____

❷ Think about what you have learnt about the history of The Bahamas. Write about at least two ways in which human rights were violated in our country's history.

_____
_____
_____
_____
_____
_____

❸ In a newspaper or news website, read about current events in The Bahamas. Identify any situations where human rights are being violated.

_____
_____
_____
_____

The rights of children

Children have some special rights. The **Convention on the Rights of the Child** is an international declaration of these rights.

* All children have the right to a name, enough food to eat and a place to live.
* All children should be looked after when they are sick.
* Children have a right to grow up with love, affection and security.
* Disabled children have a right to special treatment and education.
* All children have a right to free education, and should be protected from neglect, cruelty and exploitation.
* Nobody is allowed to make children work before a certain age.
* Children must be protected from discrimination.

1. Read this extract from the Convention on the Rights of the Child:

Article 28

1. …
   (a) Make primary education compulsory and available free to all;
   (b) Encourage the development of different forms of secondary education, including general and vocational education, make them available and accessible to every child, and take appropriate measures such as the introduction of free education and offering financial assistance in case of need;
   (c) Make higher education accessible to all on the basis of capacity by every appropriate means;
   (d) Make educational and vocational information and guidance available and accessible to all children;
   (e) Take measures to encourage regular attendance at schools and the reduction of drop-out rates.
2. States Parties shall take all appropriate measures to ensure that school discipline is administered in a manner consistent with the child's human dignity and in conformity with the present Convention.

2. Summarise Article 28 in simple language so that the meaning is easier to understand.

Unit 11 Rights and responsibilities

The right to education

Every child has the right to education. This creates many responsibilities for the government, for parents and for children themselves. The **Education Act of The Bahamas** describes the rights and responsibilities related to education.

1. Brainstorm: what do parents, governments and children have to do to make sure that children get the education to which they are entitled?

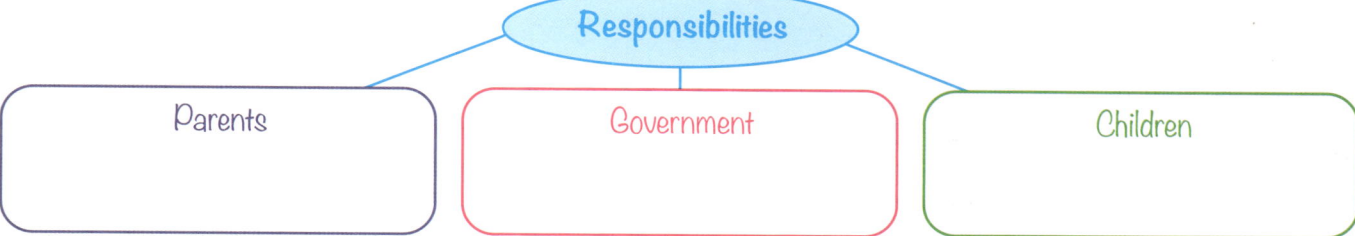

2. Find the Education Act of The Bahamas, either online or in a reference book.

   a   Which part of the Act talks about parents' rights and responsibilities in their children's education?

   b   Read this section and list three rights that parents have with respect to their child's education.

3. Explain why each statement is incorrect. Refer to the Education Act of The Bahamas.

   a   Parents have a responsibility to build schools and train teachers.

   b   The government has to provide a teacher for each family.

   c   All children must learn exactly the same things.

   d   Teachers should never speak to parents about their children's behaviour or progress.

   e   Under no circumstances may a child be educated at home.

   f   Students have the right to freedom of speech and movement. This means that they can do whatever they like at school.

Chapter 4 Government

Correctional services

All citizens have **rights** that are protected by law. They also have **responsibilities** to uphold the laws of the country. When citizens break the laws of the country, they may lose some of their rights, such as the right to freedom. They may be sent to **correctional institutions**.

1. Name the three correctional institutions found in The Bahamas:
   a for boys _____
   b for girls _____
   c for adults _____

2. Where are these institutions located? _____

3. Invite a police officer to speak to your class. Interview them about their job.

- Place of work: ....
- Working hours: ....
- Special training: ....
- Why I chose this job: ....
- Best part of the job: ....
- Toughest part of the job: ....

Add your own questions here, and fill in the answers from the interview.

....
....
....
....
....
....
....
....
....
....
....

Unit 11 Rights and responsibilities

Justice and revenge

Justice comes from the word 'just' meaning fair. **Revenge** is different to justice. Revenge usually involves harming another person to punish them for wrongdoing. Revenge can make conflicts worse. Justice aims to restore peace.

James broke Eric's Rubik's cube. So Eric tore up James' schoolbooks.

Simone broke her neighbour's window. She apologised. The neighbour accepted the apology but asked that Simone get the window fixed.

1. What difference do the stories show between justice and revenge?
   Justice _____
   Revenge _____

2. How would Eric and James' story end if Eric sought justice rather than revenge? Rewrite it with a new ending.
   _____
   _____
   _____

3. How would Simone's story end if the neighbour sought revenge rather than justice?
   _____
   _____

4. Write your own definitions of these words.

   key words

   justice _____
   revenge _____

Chapter 4 Government

Conflicts and disagreements

Conflicts and **disagreements** can occur between individual people, but they can also occur between cities or countries. When conflicts arise between bigger social groups, they can have serious consequences for many people. Current events are things that are happening at the present time. Global events are events happening around the world. Reading and listening to international news sources can keep you informed about current global events.

5. Look at a newspaper, watch a TV news broadcast, or find an online news source (print or video). Find two examples of conflicts. Write a summary of each example below. Include the location of the conflict, the countries or groups that are in conflict with each other, and the main cause or source of the conflict.

12 Our people, our heritage

CHAPTER 5: Culture

Family names in The Bahamas

Many families in The Bahamas today can trace their names back to our ancestors. For example, the surnames of some of the Eleutheran Adventurers included Bethell, Carey, Charlow, Culmer, Kemp, Sands, Watkins, Dorsett, Newbold, Ingraham, Lowe, Sawyer, Knowles and Pinder. The Loyalists settled on different islands: John Russell in Abaco; Dennis Rolle in Exuma; Robert Curry in New Providence; Alexander Collie in Crooked Island and Wyannie Malone in Hope Town. The setters were white people from Britain and America, but in the time of slavery, it was common for the enslaved people to take their owners' surnames. Therefore, many black families eventually had the same surnames as the white settlers. Today, Bahamians come from many other backgrounds too, including Greek, Chinese, Jewish and Arab heritage.

1. Do you have friends, family members or other acquaintances who have any of the surnames listed above? Write the names of people you know who have these names today.

_____
_____
_____
_____

2. Think about your family – the names of people in your family, what they look like, and the stories they tell about the past. Tick the groups that you think your ancestors may have come from.

- [ ] Lucayans
- [ ] Other Taino groups
- [ ] Spanish Europeans
- [ ] American Loyalists
- [ ] English colonists
- [ ] African enslaved people
- [ ] Chinese
- [ ] Greek
- [ ] Haitian
- [ ] Arab
- [ ] Other

3. Write more about your family background below:

_____
_____
_____
_____
_____
_____
_____
_____

Chapter 5 Culture

4. Interview your family to find out more about two of your ancestors. Try to find out about different sides of your family (for example, paternal and maternal ancestry). Write what you found out, and draw the flags of the countries they came from.

- Name of ancestor and/or relation to me: ....
....

- Reason they came to The Bahamas: ....
....
....

- The story I found out: ....

Unit 12 Our people, our heritage

- Name of ancestor and/or relation to me: ....
  ....

- Reason they came to The Bahamas: ....
  ....
  ....

- The story I found out: ....
  ....
  ....
  ....
  ....
  ....
  ....
  ....
  ....
  ....
  ....

Chapter 5 Culture

Nation builders

1 What do we mean by a 'nation builder'? Write your own definition.

key word

nation builder ....

2 In each of the boxes, write the names of people who have helped build the culture and heritage of The Bahamas.

Sports	Music	Arts

Religion	Education	Politics

Unit 12 Our people, our heritage

3. Choose someone who you see as a nation builder. It may be one of the figures from your textbook, or someone else you see as a Bahamian national symbol. Find out more about them, and complete the ⭐ fact file.

A Bahamian nation bulder

- Name: ....
- Date of birth: ....
- Place of birth: ....
  ....
- Personal history: ....
  ....
  ....
  ....
- Achievements: ....
  ....
  ....
  ....
- Why I believe this person is a nation builder:
  ....
  ....
  ....
  ....

13 Holidays and celebrations

Junkanoo instruments

1 Describe at least three things in the picture below that you will always see at Junkanoo.

_____

_____

_____

2 Below you can read the steps for making a drum, but they are all out of order. Number the steps to show the correct order.

- ☐ Stretch the soaked skin tightly over a barrel or bin.
- ☐ Heat the drum over a small fire.
- ☐ Fasten the stretched skin around the sides with small nails.
- ☐ Perform with the drum!
- ☐ Soak the skins in lime for several months.
- ☐ Leave to dry.

Musical instruments used at Junkanoo

3 What two other instruments are usually used at Junkanoo? Write their names and draw a small picture of each.

104

Junkanoo costumes

In the early days of Junkanoo, slaves would make their costumes from any materials they could find – paper and bottles, banana leaves, straw and stones. They painted their faces with powder or flour, or made masks from paper bags or sacks. Today, we usually use cardboard, glue, wire and crepe paper, and sometimes also beads, glitter and feathers.

Junkanoo costumes

1 Match each costume-making technique to the correct description.

- shingling
- fringeing
- band-aiding
- streaking

- Cutting or tearing long strips of cloth or paper into many thinner strips to make a decorative edge or border, sometimes using barber's clippers.
- Cutting short lengths of fringe and pasting them in layers, overlapping one another.
- Creating a border by sticking a band of paper or foil over a sheet of crepe paper.
- Taping over the rough edges of cardboard pieces with masking tape, or paper and glue, to make them smoother.

2 Describe two rules for Junkanoo costumes.

_____
_____
_____

3 Briefly describe how you would make a skirt or mask for Junkanoo.

_____
_____
_____

Chapter 5 Culture

Public holidays

1. Look at this list of public holidays. Discuss the holidays with a friend. What does the holiday mark – a religious celebration, a historical event or a different custom? Write the date of the holiday and a short explanation next to each one.

   - New Year's Day _____
   - Independence Day _____
   - Good Friday _____
   - Emancipation Day _____
   - Easter Monday _____
   - National Heroes Day _____
   - Whit Monday _____
   - Christmas Day _____
   - Boxing Day _____
   - Randol Fawkes Labour Day _____

2. Draw a star next to the public holidays that might usually have Junkanoo parades.

3. Which holiday…
   a is also known as Guanahani? _____
   b celebrates freedom from slavery? _____
   c marks the beginning of Pentecost? _____
   d honours the rights of workers? _____
   e celebrates the birth of Jesus Christ? _____

4. Describe some of the ways you celebrate Whit Monday in your community.

   _____

Unit 13 Holidays and celebrations

Randol Fawkes Labour Day

1 What was the full name and title of Randol Fawkes?
_____

2 When was he born? _____

3 He played many important roles. Cross out the ones that do not apply.

civil rights activist · singer · author · free trade unionist · lawyer

builder · politician · farmer · king

4 Explain what you understand by each of these terms.

key words

trade union ....

....

labour movement ....

....

5 Give two examples of labour laws and explain why think they are important.
_____
_____
_____
_____

6 Why do you think the Government of The Bahamas decided to name Labour Day after Randol Fawkes?
_____
_____
_____
_____
_____

Chapter 5 Culture

Regattas

In the past, boat building was a key survival skill for Bahamians. In the first half of the 20th century, the fleet of working sailboats was declining. In 1954, a group of yachtsmen came together to organise a regatta for Bahamian working sailing craft. The idea was that this event would give Bahamian sailors an opportunity to gather in one place, to enjoy their sport together, and also to showcase their trade and skill. It would also give the local boat builders an opportunity to upgrade the working boats. The event was so successful that it became an annual event, and inspired many other similar events throughout The Bahamas.

Bahamian man with working sailboats

1. Find out what each of these types of boats are. Draw a picture or write a short description.

Sloop

Schooner

Dinghy

Oyster dredger

Unit 13 Holidays and celebrations

❷ With a partner or group, discuss the types of activities that take place at festivals, such as Junkanoo, and at regattas. List your ideas in the table and add descriptions of the similarities and differences between festivals and regattas. Some ideas have been filled in to get you started.

Activities	Regattas	Festivals
Fancy-dress costumes		
Music		
Many people coming to watch		
Races		

❸ Make a model of a boat that might be used at a regatta. Draw your design here. Remember to add notes about the materials you will use for your model.

14 Foods and plants of The Bahamas

HINT
You can find the song on YouTube.

Dishes of The Bahamas

1 Listen to the song 'The Buffet' by Eddie Minnis.

  a As you listen to the song, write down all the foods and drinks that are mentioned in the song.

  b In your own words, write a summary of the story that the song tells.

2 Write examples of at least three different traditional Bahamian dishes, and examples of occasions where you would usually eat them.

Unit 14 Foods and plants of The Bahamas

3 What famous Bahamian dish is the person in the photograph making?

Research a good recipe for this dish, and write your recipe here.

Chapter 5 Culture

Flora of The Bahamas

The **flora** of a region are its plants and vegetation. In The Bahamas, some plants are referred to as 'bush'. Many people use bush medicine for natural remedies. We also use plants to **beautify** our homes and communities.

❶ Write your own definition of these terms.

key words

flora ....

bush ....

bush medicine ....

beautification ....

❷ Walk around your neighbourhood. You may like to take a visit to a park, botanical garden or plant nursery. List the names of plants that we use for these purposes.

Plants used to create hedges	Trees that beautify my community

Other plants used to beautify my community